# Photo Booth 101

## A COMPREHENSIVE GUIDE TO STARTING A SUCCESSFUL PHOTO BOOTH RENTAL BUSINESS

JAMES R DYLAN

www.photobooth101.com

Published by Life Images Productions, LLC

The publisher offers no warranties or guarantee that the information herein is accurate or complete and is not responsible for errors or omissions. The publisher assumes no liability for damages resulting from use of this information.

All trademarks and registered trademarks are the property of their respective holders.

Copyright © 2012 Life Images Productions, LLC

All rights reserved.

ISBN-13: 978-1479185344
ISBN-10: 1479185345

## DEDICATION

The book is dedicated to my loving family, who always supports all of my ventures.

# CONTENTS

**DEDICATION** ... III
**CONTENTS** ... V

**CHAPTER 1 - OVERVIEW OF THE PHOTO BOOTH RENTAL INDUSTRY** ... 1
   WHO RENTS PHOTO BOOTHS? ... 3
   TYPES OF PHOTO BOOTHS ... 4
      *Vintage Booth* ... 4
   HARD CASE BOOTH ... 5
      *Pipe and Drape Booth* ... 5
      *Popup Tent Booth* ... 5
      *Open Booth* ... 6
   REASONS TO START A PHOTO BOOTH RENTAL BUSINESS: ... 6
- *Relatively Low Startup Costs* ... 6
- *High Profit Potential* ... 6
- *Minimal Expertise or Training Required* ... 7
- *Rewarding Work* ... 7
- *Socially Conscious* ... 7

   THINGS TO CONSIDER BEFORE DIVING-IN HEAD FIRST: ... 7
- *Market Saturation* ... 7
- *Weekend and Evening Hours* ... 8
- *Rapidly Changing Technology* ... 8

   IS THERE A PHOTO BOOTH IN YOUR FUTURE? ... 8

**CHAPTER 2 – BUSINESS FORMATION** ... 11
   *Sole Proprietorship* ... 12
   *Partnership* ... 13
   *Limited Liability Corporation (LLC)* ... 14
   *Corporation* ... 15
   FORMS AND LICENSES ... 16

**CHAPTER 3. PHOTO BOOTH BASICS** ... 19
   PHYSICAL STRUCTURE ... 19
   CAMERA ... 20
      *DSLR* ... 20

- *Prosumer-Grade Point and Shoot* ............................................................. 20
- *Web Cam* ................................................................................................. 21
- *Picture Quality* ........................................................................................ 21
- *Video Capabilities* ................................................................................... 22
- *Complexity* .............................................................................................. 22
- *Size Constraints* ...................................................................................... 22
- *USB Support* ........................................................................................... 23
- *Power Supply* .......................................................................................... 23
- *Software Support* .................................................................................... 23
- COMPUTER SYSTEM .................................................................................... 24
  - *Laptop, Desktop or Tablet* ................................................................... 25
  - *Computer Specs (CPU, Memory, Hard Drive Space)* ......................... 25
  - *External Ports* ...................................................................................... 25
  - *Operating System* ................................................................................ 26
- BOOTH SOFTWARE ...................................................................................... 26
  - *PhotoBoof* ............................................................................................ 26
  - *Breeze Systems Photo Booth Software* ............................................... 27
  - *Spark Booth* ......................................................................................... 27
  - *SnapShot Studio* ................................................................................... 27
- MONITOR ..................................................................................................... 28
- PRINTER ...................................................................................................... 28
  - *Dye Subliminal* .................................................................................... 29
  - *Photo Inkjet* ......................................................................................... 29
- LIGHTING .................................................................................................... 30
- OTHER ACCESSORIES .................................................................................. 30
  - *Props* .................................................................................................... 30
  - *Guestbook* ............................................................................................ 31
  - *Backdrops* ............................................................................................ 31
  - *Blue/Green Screens* ............................................................................. 31
  - *Decorative Lighting* ............................................................................. 31
- ESTIMATED TOTAL BOOTH COST ................................................................ 32

## CHAPTER 4 – UNDERSTANDING YOUR MARKET .......................... 33

- CHOOSING YOUR TERRITORY ..................................................................... 33
- GET TO KNOW YOUR MARKET ................................................................... 35
  - *Wedding Market* ................................................................................... 35
  - *Bar/Bat Mitzvah Market* ...................................................................... 36
  - *School Market* ...................................................................................... 37
  - *Party Market* ........................................................................................ 37
  - *Corporate Market* ................................................................................ 37

GET TO KNOW YOUR COMPETITION ..................................................38
CHOOSING YOUR NICHE ....................................................................39
DECIDING YOUR PRICE-RANGE ..........................................................40
    *Why it Pays to be Good* ..................................................................*40*
    *Why it Pays to be Cheap* ................................................................*41*
    *The Middle Ground* .......................................................................*41*

**CHAPTER 5 – OBTAINING YOUR FIRST BOOTH .................43**

BUILD VS. BUY ..................................................................................43
QUESTIONS TO ASK BEFORE BUYING A BOOTH? .................................45
    *What are the dimensions and how much does it weigh?* .............*45*
    *How long does it take to setup?* .....................................................*46*
    *What equipment is included?* ........................................................*46*
    *Is Software Included?* ....................................................................*46*
    *What type of camera does it use?* .................................................*46*
    *What type of printer does it use?* ..................................................*46*
    *Can it be customized?* ...................................................................*47*
    *Does it come with a warrantee?* ...................................................*47*
    *Is technical support provided?* ......................................................*47*
BUILDING A PVC PIPE BOOTH ..........................................................47
BUILDING AN ALUMINUM PIPE BOOTH .............................................49
ELECTRONICS ENCLOSURES ..............................................................51
TRANSPORTING YOUR EQUIPMENT ....................................................52
    *Cases* ..............................................................................................*52*
    *Carts* ..............................................................................................*53*
BACKUP EQUIPMENT ........................................................................53

**CHAPTER 6 - DEVELOPING YOUR PACKAGES AND PRICES ...........55**

GOLD, SILVER, BRONZE ....................................................................55
    *The Bronze Package - $695* ..........................................................*56*
    *The Silver Package - $895* ............................................................*56*
    *The Gold Package - $1095* ...........................................................*56*
ALA CARTE ......................................................................................57
HOURLY RATES ................................................................................58
HYBRID PACKAGES WITH ADD-ONS ..................................................59
    *The Bronze Package - $195 Per Hour* .........................................*59*
    *The Silver Package - $295 Per Hour* ...........................................*59*
    *The Gold Package - $395 Per Hour* .............................................*60*
    *Extra Features* ...............................................................................*60*

**CHAPTER 7 – CONTRACTS .........................................................61**

- Business Information ... 62
- Client Information ... 62
- Event Date and Times ... 63
- Venue Information ... 63
- Package and Price Information ... 63
- Arrival Time ... 64
- Permission and Accommodations ... 64
- Technical Difficulties ... 64
- Failure to Comply ... 64
- Liability ... 65
- Copyright ... 65
- Modifications ... 65
- Jurisdiction ... 65
- Cancellation ... 65
- Deposits ... 66
- Subtotal/Total Calculation ... 66
- Balance Due ... 66
- Signatures ... 66
- SAMPLE PHOTO BOOTH RENTAL AGREEMENT ... 66

## CHAPTER 8 - DESIGNING YOUR WEBSITE ... 71

- DOMAIN NAME ... 71
- HOSTING ... 72
- WEBSITE DESIGN ... 72
- PACKAGES AND PRICES ... 73
- SAMPLE PHOTOS ... 73
- ABOUT US PAGE ... 74
- CONTACT ... 74
- ONLINE BOOKING ... 75
- SEARCH ENGINE OPTIMIZATION ... 75
  - Descriptive Title and Description ... 76
  - Use keywords in your Page Content ... 76
  - Write a Blog ... 76
  - List Your Site in Directories ... 77
  - Write a Press Release ... 78

## CHAPTER 9 - SELLING YOUR BOOTH ... 79

- SALES PITCH ... 79
- RESPONDING TO EMAIL INQUIRIES ... 80
- FIELDING INCOMING PHONE CALLS ... 82
- FOLLOW-UPS ... 84

DEPOSITS/CONTRACTS .................................................................... 85

## CHAPTER 10 – ADVERTISING ................................................. 87

ONLINE ............................................................................................. 87
   *Wedding and Event Vendor Directories* ............................................ 87
   *Search Engine Advertising (Pay per Click)* ....................................... 89
   *Social Media* ..................................................................................... 90
   *Coupon Sites* ..................................................................................... 91
OFFLINE ........................................................................................... 92
   *Bridal and Event Magazines* ............................................................ 92
   *Direct Mail* ........................................................................................ 92
   *Bridal Expos* ...................................................................................... 93
   *Word of Mouth* .................................................................................. 93
   *Partnering With other Vendors* ........................................................ 93

## CHAPTER 11 - EVENT PREPARATIONS .................................. 95

REVIEW THE CONTRACT ..................................................................... 95
SCHEDULE TRAVEL AND SETUP TIME .................................................. 96
EQUIPMENT TESTING .......................................................................... 97
THINGS TO BRING ............................................................................... 97
GOING OVER THE CHECKLIST .............................................................. 99

## CHAPTER 12 - LAUNCHING ..................................................... 103

PLANNING A DRY RUN ..................................................................... 103
PRESS RELEASE ................................................................................ 105
ADVERTISING CAMPAIGN .................................................................. 106
   *Copywriting* .................................................................................... 106
   *Measuring Results* .......................................................................... 107

## CHAPTER 13 - MANAGING YOUR BUSINESS ....................... 109

ACCOUNTING ................................................................................... 109
EMPLOYEES ...................................................................................... 110
FINANCES ......................................................................................... 112

## CHAPTER 14 - CUSTOMER SERVICE ..................................... 115

PROFESSIONAL COMMUNICATIONS .................................................... 115
AVOIDING MISUNDERSTANDINGS ...................................................... 117
DEALING WITH AN UNHAPPY CUSTOMER ......................................... 118

## CHAPTER 15 - EXPANDING YOUR BUSINESS ...................... 121

MULTIPLE BOOTHS ........................................................................... 121

EXPANDING YOUR TERRITORY ........................................................................ 122
OFFERING ADDITIONAL SERVICES ................................................................ 123
**CONCLUSION** ............................................................................................**125**

# Chapter 1 - Overview of the Photo Booth Rental Industry

The Photo booth dates back as far as 1889, when French inventor, T. E. Enjalbert debuted it at the World's Fair in Paris. Although his machine was not an immediate commercial success, it paved the way for a long evolution of technologies over the course of the next century.

Over the next hundred years, photo booths became extremely popular throughout Europe in places such as shopping malls, train stations and on busy streets, where they were used primarily for practical purposes such as taking photos for passports or driver's licenses. The United States saw its share of Photo booths as well, however, Americans perceived them as more of a novelty item, and they were more often placed in locations associated with fun, such as boardwalks, arcades and amusement parks. Many of us still to this day have fond memories of cramming into these clunky old machines with our friends, making silly faces, and waiting what seemed like forever for the low-quality negatives to develop.

With the advent of technology, we have overcome many of the limitations of these wonderful old-time machines. Most modern photo booths are comprised completely of digital technology. Still, that happy-go-lucky spirit of the good old-fashioned booth lives on in many of us every time we step through the curtains, and there's a whole new generation of photo booth enthusiasts who are re-inventing the timeless tradition.

This enthusiasm, along with the compactness and relative inexpensiveness of digital technology, has inspired entrepreneurs of today to develop high-tech, easily-transportable photo booths, pioneering a new industry: the photo booth rental business.

As far as we can tell, this movement can be traced to the late 1990's, when the owners of the *Minnesota State Fair Penny Arcade* developed a transportable photo booth and began renting it out to local weddings and events. Today they operate under the business name Photo Booth Memories, and are often credited as being the first photo booth rental company. A huge success, the idea caught on like wildfire, and quickly spread to other parts of the country.

Today, there are well over 1000 photo booth rental companies operating in the US. Below is a table showing the results of a 2012 survey estimating the number of photo booth rental companies operating in the top 20 US metropolitan markets.

| City, State | Photo Booth Rental Companies |
|---|---|
| Los Angeles, CA | 67 |
| Chicago, IL | 62 |
| Dallas, TX | 55 |
| Detroit, MI | 53 |

| Miami, FL | 43 |
|---|---|
| Houston, TX | 38 |
| Boston, MA | 36 |
| San Francisco, CA | 34 |
| St. Paul, MN | 31 |
| New Orleans, LA | 31 |
| Austin, TX | 31 |
| Washington DC | 29 |
| New York, NY | 24 |
| Philadelphia, PA | 24 |
| Atlanta, GE | 24 |
| San Antonio, TX | 24 |
| San Diego, CA | 22 |
| Kansas City, MO | 22 |
| Phoenix, AZ | 19 |
| Seattle, WA | 10 |

## Who Rents Photo Booths?

Probably the first and still one of the most common places to find a photo booth rental is at a wedding. These customers are couples getting married who want something fun to entertain their guests, while at the same time giving them a unique keepsake to take home. Additionally, wedding photo booths often offer a guestbook to collect a copy of all of the photo strips, in which friends and family can sign and express their well-wishes. Weddings can provide a steady stream of revenue to a photo booth rental business due to the fact that people get married all year round, and weddings are the one event where people really open up their wallets.

In addition to weddings, other types of events where people rent photo booths include: Bar/Bat Mitzvahs, Proms, Dances, Birthday Parties, Graduation Parties, Anniversary Parties, etc. The popularity of photo booths at these types of events is exploding, whether they are held in traditional banquet halls, large venues, fire halls, or even in backyards and living rooms. These events are gaining a significant percentage of the overall photo booth rental market share, and for many companies make up the lion's share.

Another, new and exciting photo booth rental customer is corporate America. Businesses small and large spend a lot of money wooing clients at corporate parties and conventions, and they are starting to get in on the photo booth action as well. These events range from large corporate dinners, cocktail parties, lunch meetings, to booths setup to draw people's attention at trade shows.

Even Uncle Sam has been known to call on local photo booth vendors from time to time. Photo booths are popping up at government-sponsored festivals, job fairs, conferences, award ceremonies and more.

## Types of Photo Booths

Below are some of the most common types of photo booths being rented today and some of the pros and cons of each for comparison.

**Vintage Booth**
The "Vintage" or sometimes "Classic" photo booth is either an authentic or replica of the original photo booths found at boardwalks and amusement parks of the 50's, 60's, 70's and 80's. Some employ original chemical/film processing, although most have been converted to digital. Generally, these are fixed or modular units constructed of steel, wood, and/or fiberglass. They are usually quite heavy (400-800 lb), and measure roughly 3ft wide, 4ft long, and 6ft high. Most have either a small bench or one or two round cushioned seats inside. These photo booths have the appeal of being charming, and embodying the full

nostalgic spirit of the original photo booths, but they are the most expensive variety, difficult to transport, and typically can only hold 2-4 people at a time.

## Hard Case Booth

The "Hard Case" booth is a fixed or modular booth with a hard case surrounding, usually made from either fiberglass or particle board. They are typically slightly larger than the Vintage booths, and often employ a more modern, high-tech design. These booths may be considered less authentic than the Vintage booths, but are generally somewhat less expensive to purchase or build, and can often accommodate slightly more people inside (typically 4-6).

## Pipe and Drape Booth

The "Pipe and Drape" photo booth is an inexpensive and streamlined design, which is becoming the de facto photo booth variety for most weddings and private events. It generally consists of a roughly 4ft wide, 6ft long, and 6ft high cube frame constructed of either aluminum or PVC pipes, with curtains hung around the exterior to form a private space with folding chairs inside. Generally, a camera and monitor are fixed inside the booth (either on a table or within a portable unit), and a printer may be setup either inside or outside of the booth. These booths are significantly less expensive than the Vintage or Hard Case variety, and may be considered by some purist to be somewhat tacky or cheap. Nonetheless, they have the advantages of being easier to transport and assemble, and can usually fit much more people inside (as many as 6-10). For these reasons, along with the reduced price, the Pipe and Drape photo booth is a very popular choice these days.

## Popup Tent Booth

Another inexpensive and quick-to-deploy option is the "popup tent" photo booth. These consist of a self-erecting polyester tent, with lightweight fiberglass poles that can be quickly expanded or collapsed. Similar to the Pipe and Drape booth, the camera and monitor are typically setup inside the tent, with the printer either in or outside. These booths have the advantage of being light, extremely easy to transport and setup, but are typically smaller than the Pipe and Drape booths, and are somewhat less sturdy – occasionally collapsing at inopportune times with guests inside, which could either be received with light laughter or complete anger depending on how forgiving the customer is. Generally, this is a fast and cheap solution, but not the first choice for most customers.

**Open Booth**
The "Open Booth" or sometimes "Open Air Booth" is the simplest form of photo booth, and is actually becoming a very popular choice for events held at smaller venues or in homes, as well as for customers who are on a budget. Generally, it is not a booth at all, but simply a camera, monitor and printer, either setup on a table or contained within a portable unit, usually with some sort of simple backdrop setup in the background. Although these lack the element of cramming people into a small space, people nonetheless still truly enjoy the experience and can receive the same quality photo strips, generally for a significantly lower price.

## Reasons to Start a Photo Booth Rental Business:
- **Relatively Low Startup Costs**- Depending on the style of photo booth that you select and the number of features and amenities you plan to offer, typical startup costs to begin operating your first booth range from about $5,000-$15,000. Compared to other business ventures, this is a relatively small initial investment, and if all goes well the payback is fairly quick. With a good business plan, and a lot of hard work and commitment, you can reasonably expect to reach a break-even point within the first 6 months to a year, or even sooner.

- **High Profit Potential-** With the right pricing strategy and strong marketing, a photo booth rental business can be highly profitable. Whereas a typical retail business may have a profit margin of about 7%-12%, a photo booth rental business can potentially earn much higher figures. A 30%-60% profit is not uncommon.

- **Minimal Expertise or Training Required** - Unlike many fields that require years of training, special talents and skills, or hard-to-come-by credentials, just about anyone is capable of operating a photo booth. The essential traits that will decide your success are your ambition, communication skills, and work ethic.

- **Rewarding Work** - Operating a photo booth is very rewarding work because it mostly entails standing by and watching people have the time of their life. It is also quite rewarding to own a successful business, and a photo booth rental business is a business with a real potential for success.

- **Socially Conscious** - Unfortunately, many businesses today operate in ways that have unintended consequences (pollution, health problems, political controversies, etc.). If you are concerned about these problems, you'll be comforted to know that a photo booth rental business has a small carbon footprint, and minimal negative social or environmental impact.

## Things to Consider Before Diving-In Head First:
- **Market Saturation** - Because of the relatively low cost-of-entry and other benefits mentioned above, some markets may be getting saturated with photo booth rental

startups, and competition in your area may be tough. It is important to thoroughly research the market in your region before making the decision to go forward, and make sure to take this into consideration when choosing your territory and niche. You may find it necessary to offer your services to a broader market, and be willing to travel to neighboring markets. You may also need to be more creative in your marketing, perhaps carving out a niche or specialty to differentiate yourself from your competitors.

- **Weekend and Evening Hours** - Most likely, your photo booth rental business will be servicing Weddings, Bar/Bat Mitzvahs, Birthday Parties and similar events. More often than not, these events are held on Friday nights and the weekends. This means, if you are going to be working the events yourself, you will need to be willing to give up most of your weekends. At first it may seem like a small sacrifice, but after months of "all work and no play", you may start to question if the price is too high. It is important to give this serious consideration before starting your business and assess the impact this will have on your family and social life.

- **Rapidly Changing Technology** - Photo booths are evolving rapidly and the technology surrounding them is changing every year. In order for your photo booth rental business to stay relevant and survive, it will be essential to stay abreast of these innovations and be willing to make investments in the latest technology to keep your equipment up-to-date.

## Is there a Photo Booth in Your Future?
The photo booth has a rich history dating back over a hundred

years, and today the photo booth rental industry is thriving. The barriers to entry into the market are low, and the demand for photo booth rentals is growing. There are several different types of booths to choose from and a huge variety of features and amenities to make your booth unique. Like any business, success depends on planning, hard work, dedication and a little bit of luck. Do you think you have what it takes? If so, please continue reading. In the following chapters we will outline everything you need to know to form your business, design and/or purchase your first booth, market your services, and build a framework from which you can continue to run a successful operation.

JAMES R DYLAN

# Chapter 2 – Business Formation

Once you have made the decision to start your own photo booth rental business, one of the first things you will need to do is to decide on the legal structure for your company and complete the necessary forms and paperwork to register your business. Below is an overview of the four most common types of business structures used by photo booth rental companies in the US, and some information on how to form each one.

Please note this overview provides general information regarding each business type; however, there are many details which may vary from state to state. Additionally, many municipalities require additional registrations, business licenses, etc. not discussed here. Be sure to research the requirements in your municipality and state before beginning the process. See the Forms and Licenses section below for links to online resources to help you get started. You may wish to seek professional advice from an attorney, accountant or financial specialist to assist you in determining the best business structure for your needs.

Disclaimer: This section is provided for informational purposes only. Although some opinions are expressed, this should not be construed as legal or financial advice.

## Sole Proprietorship

A sole proprietorship is the simplest and most common business type. It is essentially a single individual who is in business for his or her self.

Sole proprietorships have the advantages of being easy and inexpensive to form, but they are not suitable for businesses that have more than one owner. Furthermore, when conducting business as a sole proprietor, the individual who owns the business assumes full legal responsibility for the activities of the business, and can be held personally liable for any lawsuits or claims against the business. Although photo booth rental businesses are not particularly prone to legal problems, there is always a risk that something could go wrong at an event. For example, someone may trip and fall inside the booth or you or one of your employees may accidentally damage property at a venue. It is important to give this careful consideration before choosing to do business as a sole proprietorship. If you feel that personal liability may be an issue, you may prefer to form your business as an LLC or corporation instead.

If the business has a name other than the name of the individual who owns it, then a fictitious name or DBA (doing business as) must be registered. This is usually registered with the state, and there is generally a small fee (typically $50-$100). Every state and municipality varies as to what additional forms and/or licenses must be filed to do business within their jurisdictions. Please see the Forms and Licenses section below for some helpful online resources to get started.

## Partnership

A partnership is a business consisting of two or more owners who share in the decision making for the business. The key element of a business partnership is a legally binding Partnership Agreement between all parties who will share a stake in the business. At a minimum, it is essential that this document cover in detail how business decisions will be made, what each partner's responsibilities entail, how profits (or losses) will be split, and how conflicts will be resolved. You may choose to retain an attorney to assist with the drafting of this document or write one yourself. There are many free Partnership Agreement templates available online as well to help you get started.

Partnerships may be less expensive or easier to form than LLC's or corporations depending on legal fees and the administrative burdens of your particular municipality or state. However, there are several drawbacks to consider when going with this option. As is the case with a sole proprietorship, partnerships do not provide legal protection from liability if the company gets sued. This means that you and/or any partners can be held personally liable for damages. Additionally, partnerships can get messy when there's a dispute between partners. Depending on how well thought out and detailed the Partnership Agreement is, there is a potential risk of litigation if and when partners fail to agree on something. These are all things to consider when forming a partnership. To avoid these problems, many people opt for either an LLC or corporation.

Like a sole proprietorship, partnerships generally must register a fictitious name with the state, and will likely need to register with various state and municipal offices and/or obtain licenses. Please see the Forms and Licenses section below for some helpful online resources to get started.

## Limited Liability Corporation (LLC)

A Limited Liability Corporation or LLC is special type of corporation, which attempts to provide small businesses with the same benefits as a standard corporation, but without imposing as many administrative and tax burdens. In most states, LLCs may consist of one or multiple owners, which are referred to as members.

Unlike a sole proprietorship or partnership, an LLC is a legal business entity separate from the people who own and operate the business. LLCs are desirable because of the concept of limited liability, which provides the business owners with a layer of protection in the event that the business is sued, and shields personal assets from those seeking damages. LLCs are also advantageous over general partnerships because cut-and-dry remedies for many of the common disputes that occur between partners are built into the legal framework of the LLC, making it less likely for litigation to become necessary and making it easier for courts to rule when litigation does occur.

Forming an LLC primarily consists of filing a form known as Articles of Organization with the state in which you wish to register your business. This is typically a straightforward form which can be obtained from the state and requires a fee to be filed (usually $100-$300). You may either complete this form on your own or for an additional fee use a filing service to assist you.

If your LLC will consist of multiple members, you will also need to complete an Operating Agreement. An Operating Agreement is similar to a Partnership Agreement as it outlines individual responsibilities, how profits (or losses) will be split, etc. You may be able to obtain an Operating Agreement template from your state, from a filing service or by searching online.

Please refer to the Forms and Licenses section below for more helpful online resources.

## Corporation

A corporation is a legal entity formed to conduct business or other activities. Corporations can have one or many owners who are often referred to as shareholders. Corporations are controlled by officers and/or directors who are appointed by the shareholders (who may also be one in the same).

There are several advantages to forming a corporation over other business structures. First of all, ownership and control is easily determined by the number of shares held in the corporation, which generally dictates the percentage of the corporation that is owned and establishes the shareholder's voting rights. Of course, the main advantage to forming a corporation, which also applies to LLCs, is the concept of limited liability, which limits a person's liability to whatever they have invested in the corporation. As discussed above in the section on LLCs, this protects the business owner's personal assets from claims against the business. Corporations are slightly more difficult to form than LLCs and can get tricky when it comes to taxes.

Forming a corporation requires filing Articles of Incorporation with the state in which you wish to register your business. Additionally, depending on the state, several other forms and documents may be required. You may either complete these forms and documents on your own or for an additional fee use a filing service to assist you.

Deciding between a corporation or LLC requires some careful

examination of the specific regulations in the state where you are registering. Please refer to the Forms and Licenses section below for more helpful online resources.

Business Type Comparison

|  | Sole Proprietorship | Partnership | LLC | Corporation |
|---|---|---|---|---|
| Difficulty to form | Easy | Moderate | Slightly Difficult | Somewhat Difficult |
| Expense to form | $50-$100 | $50-$100 | $300-$600 | $300-$600 |
| Number of owners | 1 | More than 1 | 1 or more | 1 or more |
| Limited Liability | No | No | Yes | Yes |
| Taxes | Personal tax return | Personal tax return | Personal or Corporate | Corporate Taxes |

## Forms and Licenses

Once you have chosen a business structure for your company, the next step in the process of forming your business is to visit the websites of your state and municipality to find out where and how your business needs to registered and what (if any) licenses need to be obtained. A very good online reference is the Small Business Administration (www.sba.gov) website. This site has a search tool to help you identify what registration requirements are applicable in your area, and provides links to the appropriate state and municipal offices.

For sole proprietorships and partnerships you will likely need to file a fictitious name or DBA (doing business as) with the state. For LLCs and corporations, you will need to file either Articles of Organization or Articles of Incorporation. Depending on the state and municipality, you may need to register your business to collect sales tax and/or obtain other licenses.

Additionally, you will need a tax id number in order to file your federal income tax return. The IRS allows sole proprietors the option of requesting a unique tax id number (also known as an Employer ID Number or EIN) for the business or simply using the social security number of the individual who owns the business. To obtain a tax id number, visit the IRS website (www.irs.gov) and look for the link to Apply for an EIN Online. The request only takes a few minutes and your tax id number will be issued instantly.

If you are considering an LLC or corporation, you may wish to take advantage of a business filing service. These companies can make the registration process faster and easier by allowing you to submit all of your information online in a single application, and then they file the necessary forms on your behalf. Additionally, these companies often provide boilerplate templates to assist you with completing required corporate documents, and offer other services such as registered agent and mail forwarding. Below are some links to a few reputable business filing services.

It is worth mentioning that in some circumstances it is advantageous to register your LLC or corporation with a state other than the one where your business is based. Many people choose to register in states like Delaware or Nevada because these states offer lower taxes and are generally thought to be more corporation-friendly. However, in the case of a photo booth rentals business, chances are most of your business will be conducted within one state (possibly one or two neighboring states), and you will likely be required to register your business in that state anyway. Also, when registering your business out of state you will need to maintain a mailing address. Most small business use a re-mailing service for this, which is an additional yearly expense. In many cases registering in your home state will make life easier. If you are considering registering your business in a foreign state, you may wish to seek the advice of an attorney, accountant or financial advisor for more information.

Links:

Small Business Administration  http://www.sba.gov

Internal Revenue Service   http://www.irs.gov

Harvard Business Services  https://www.delawareinc.com

Biz Filings            http://www.bizfilings.com

Legal Zoom           http://www.legalzoom.com

# Chapter 3. Photo Booth Basics

This chapter provides an overview of the basic photo booth elements and their functions. There is a great deal of variation between the different types of booths discussed in Chapter one and each type has many attributes to be customized. However, with the exception of true antique vintage booths, which may rely on film and chemicals, pretty much all booths consist of the following components. If you are planning to purchase a pre-constructed booth or kit, many of these items may already be included. Otherwise, if you are building your booth from scratch, or assembling one and customizing it, you will need to give careful thought as to what type of equipment to deploy.

## Physical Structure

The Physical Structure is what makes the booth a booth. In the case of a Vintage or Hard Case booth, this may be a single unit that gets wheeled in and out of the venue or a set of modular walls, which can be broken down and reassembled onsite. In a Pipe and Drape setup, this would include the bases, poles, connectors and drapes. The one booth variety that may not have any physical structure is an Open Booth, although these usually include at least a table and possibly a backdrop. This topic is discussed in greater detail in chapter 5, including some detailed designs and comparisons of each type.

## Camera

The camera is arguably the most important element of the photo booth, as this is the device that actual captures people's photos. There are basically three types of cameras, which are commonly utilized by photo booths today. We discuss each type below and then discuss the major factors you should consider when selecting the best camera for you.

## DSLR

DSLR (Digital single-lens reflex) cameras are high-end professional cameras, which generally use interchangeable lenses. These cameras are capable of producing extraordinary photos; however, they are generally the most expensive camera option and they are also generally the most complex to configure and use. When considering this option for use in a photo booth you should be aware that the lenses are often sold separately from the camera body, and you will likely need to purchase add-on accessories to make it work.

## Prosumer-Grade Point and Shoot

The term "prosumer" refers to cameras that are somewhere in the middle between professional grade and consumer grade in quality. This group includes cameras such as the Canon Powershot series, the Nikon COOLPIX series or the Panasonic Lumix Compact series. These cameras typically do not match the quality of a DSLR camera, but with proper lighting and the right setup, they can produce photos that are actually quite good. These cameras are not cheap, but are less expensive than their DSLR big brothers, and they are generally less complex and easier to use.

## Web Cam

Web Cams are cameras that are designed to be connected to a computer, primarily for applications such as video chat or online gaming. These cameras are generally quite inexpensive and typically produce relatively low quality images. They do however have some advantages when used in a photo booth setting because of the fact that they are designed primarily to integrate with a computer. These cameras may be easier to setup and work better with some photo booth software applications than DSLRs or prosumer-grade Point and Shoot cameras.

Here are some factors to consider when making your decision:

## Picture Quality

The type of camera you choose will have a significant impact on the quality of your pictures. Obviously, people want the highest quality possible, but the fact of the matter is many photo booths today operate with relatively inexpensive cameras and as a result some produce somewhat mediocre quality photos. For many photo booth rental businesses this is acceptable. Keep in mind that the photos on the printouts are usually quite small (usually 2 inch by 6 inch strips), and many patrons are going into the photo booth just to have fun, not necessarily to get phenomenal quality pictures.

It really comes down to a business decision, which you must carefully weigh. If you are marketing your services at the high end of the price spectrum for your area, and/or branding your company as a "high quality" or "Premier" photo booth, then it may be justified to invest the money in a professional-grade DSLR camera. On the other hand, if you are in the low to medium price range, and perhaps branding yourself as the "fun" or "whacky" photo booth, then it may make more business sense to buy a "prosumer" grade camera or even a web cam.

## Video Capabilities

Many photo booths today offer the option to record short video messages, which get burned to a DVD for the host or posted to the Internet. As of the writing of this book, the jury is out as to whether this feature will be just another passing fad or an absolute must have. However, if this is something you would like to include as one of your services, make sure that the camera you select supports video.

## Complexity

DSLR cameras are designed for professional photographers, and often include hundreds of advanced features and settings. Some prosumer-grade Point and Shoot cameras are similarly complex. When used in a photo booth, chances are the majority of these features will not be applicable, and may in fact become an inconvenience. There is a high learning curve to understand what all of the settings do, and you may find yourself in a jam if you accidentally press a wrong button and the camera begins acting funny at an event. When selecting a camera, it is important to evaluate the complexity of the device and think about how difficult it may be to operate. If you don't feel comfortable with high-tech gadgets, advanced menus and settings, and so on, you may want to avoid DSLRs or some of the more advanced Point and Shoots.

## Size Constraints

The size of the camera may be important if you will be mounting the camera within an enclosure or in a confined space. Make sure that the camera is not too big or too heavy for the setup. DSLR cameras can be relatively large, Prosumer Point and Shoots are typically somewhat smaller and web cams are usually compact. Think about the design of your booth, how and where the camera will be setup, and make sure that the camera will fit and is properly mounted to be secure and sturdy.

## USB Support

In most photo booth setups, the camera will need to be connected to a computer to interact with the photo booth software. Typically, this will be via a USB connection. When selecting a camera, make sure that the camera has a USB output and is capable of being connected to a computer. Also, check to make sure that your operating system is supported.

## Power Supply

Most DSLR and Prosumer Point and Shoot Cameras are designed to run primarily off of battery power. Depending on the type and size of the battery pack, and the rate at which photographs are taken, most of these cameras can operate for anywhere from 30 minutes to a few hours. In a busy photo booth setting, the camera and flash will be working constantly, and using a significant amount of energy. If the camera is operating off of a battery pack, the power will become drained quite quickly. Instead, it is highly recommended that you use AC power. Not all cameras have AC power support, and others require the AC adapter to be purchased separately. Make sure that the camera you purchase has the ability to plugged-in, and if the adapter is not included, make sure to you can find one before buying the camera.

**Software Support** – It is important to make sure that the camera you purchase is compatible with your computer and photo booth software (and vice versa). Most photo booth software vendors provide a list of supported cameras. You may also want to perform a quick Internet search on the specific camera model and software application and possibly check in forums to see if anyone has reported bugs or performance problems with a given combination.

The chart below summarizes the information above to provide you with an overall comparison of the camera options at a glance.

|  | DSLR | Prosumer | Web Cam |
|---|---|---|---|
| Expense | $800+ | $200-$600 | $25-$75 |
| Picture Quality | High | Medium | Low |
| Video Capabilities | Varies | Varies | Yes |
| Complexity | Complex | Medium | Easy |
| USB Support | Varies | Most Supported | Most Supported |
| Size | Large | Medium | Small |
| Power Supply | Varies | Varies | USB |
| Software Support | Varies | Varies | Most Supported |

## Computer System

In a modern-day digital photo booth, there needs to be some type of computer to control the camera and printer, and power the photo booth software application. This may be a portable laptop, a small desktop computer or possibly a tablet. Here are some considerations to take into account when selecting a computer system for your Booth.

### Laptop, Desktop or Tablet

The first factor to narrow down the selection is the size and portability of the device. The majority of photo booth rental companies prefer to use laptops because they are compact, lightweight and durable. Small Desktops or Towers can be used as well, but they generally take up more space and are not typically designed to be transported. Another potential solution, which is slowly gaining in popularity, is a tablet such as an iPad or Android device. These systems have the advantage of being extremely light and compact, and have a camera and monitor built-in; however, there are not as many software choices available for these devices at this time, the screens are small, and the picture quality may be disappointing. Also, most tablets do not have ports to connect external devices like printers, so you would need to select a printer capable of using Bluetooth or Wi-Fi, which may be more expensive and difficult to find.

### Computer Specs (CPU, Memory, Hard Drive Space)

Generally, most photo booth software applications do not require excessive computer power. Most off-the-shelf laptops or Desktops will be suitable. Check with the photo booth software vendor to find out if there are minimum system requirements for CPU, Memory and Hard Drive Space. As of the writing of this book, a typical system to run a photo booth would have a dual core CPU (1.6 GHz or higher), at least 2 GB or RAM, and at least 120 GB of hard drive space to store the event photos. This type of system should be relatively easy to find and inexpensive in today's market.

### External Ports

Unless you are using a tablet or going wireless, you need to be mindful that the necessary ports to connect the camera, printer, and external monitor are available. Cameras and Printers typically use a USB port, and monitors usually use either a VGA or DVI output (sometimes HDMI). Many laptops only have one or two USB ports and not all have external monitor ports. Make sure that the laptop you purchase has adequate ports to support your other devices. It's a good idea to find one with at least four available USB ports, even if you don't have a need them right away, as you may wish to add additional devices in the future.

**Operating System**
Most photo booth software applications are developed to run on either Windows or Macintosh operating systems (or both). There may be a few out there running on Linux. When deciding an operating system, the most important thing is that you feel comfortable using it. The last thing you want to happen is to have a computer problem in the middle of an event and not know how to restart the program or reboot. If you are comfortable on PC's then go with a Windows OS; if you are more of a MAC person then go with that. There are plenty of photo booth software packages available for either platform, and many have versions that run on both.

**Booth Software**
There are several photo booth software suites available that power the user interface in which the patrons and/or photo booth attendant interact. These programs typically control everything including the onscreen menus, the camera and the printer. An Internet search and/or a visit to a photo booth forum is the best way to learn more information about these programs. Below are a few of the most popular choices and a quick review of each one.

## PhotoBoof

PhotoBoof was one of the first and is considered by many to be one of the best photo booth software suites. It is currently only available for the Windows operating system, and it is one of the most expensive options; The software is easy to use, reliable, feature-rich and supports a wide range of cameras and printers. For more information visit http://www.photoboof.com

## Breeze Systems Photo Booth Software

Breeze Systems Photo Booth software is another popular, highly regarded photo booth software suites. It is supported on both Windows and Mac, and is significantly less expensive than PhotoBoof. The application is straightforward and easy to use and has a fairly strong feature list. It supports most Canon and Nikon DSLRs, the Canon Powershot series, and most web cams. For more information visit http://breezesys.com/Photobooth

## Spark Booth

Spark Booth is an inexpensive photo booth software application, which is perhaps geared more towards home-made photo booths than professionals. It is easy to use and has some nice features, and is available for Windows or MAC. It does not support DSLR or Prosumer Point and Shoot cameras – only web cams. For more information visit http://sparkbooth.com/

## SnapShot Studio

SnapShot Studio is a newer, quite promising photo booth software suite. It is fairly expensive and because it is new may have some bugs. Nonetheless, it is feature-rich, has an excellent user interface, and supports Web Cams or DSLR cameras. For more information visit http://www.allenchristopher.com/

The chart below summarizes the information above to provide

you with an overall comparison of the software options at a glance.

|  | PhotoBoof | Breeze Systems | Spark Booth | SnapShot Studio |
|---|---|---|---|---|
| Cost | High | Medium | Low | High |
| Ease of Use | Easy | Medium | Easy | Medium |
| Features | High | Medium | Low | High |
| OS | Windows | Windows or Mac | Windows or Mac | Windows or Mac |
| Camera Support | High | Medium | Web Cam Only | Medium |

## Monitor

An important feature of most photo booths is a monitor to display the photo booth software user interface, and to show a camera preview prior to taking photos. Depending on the design of the booth, and desired user experience this might be a small tablet screen, a standard LCD computer monitor or a large plasma or LCD TV. The monitor may be mounted inside an enclosure or simply positioned on a tabletop inside the booth. Many booths also employ an additional monitor outside of the booth for people waiting in line to see the photos as they're taken. This could also be displayed on a large screen or wall outside the booth using a projector.

Many photo booths make use of touch screen interfaces where the users touch the monitor to begin taking photos, while others use buttons or have the attendant control things from a laptop setup outside. If you decide on a touch screen interface, you will need to purchase a touch screen monitor.

## Printer

The printer is an important element, as most photo booths provide patrons with instant printouts of their photo session. In most setups, the software will take 4 photos and print two copies of each on a 4X6 printout, which is then cut in half to give the guest two 2X6 strips. There are a few different options for printers, which are discussed below.

## Dye Subliminal

Dye Subliminal printers are very high quality photo printers, which use heat to transfer dye onto special photo paper. They are fast, reliable and they produce extremely high quality printouts. These printers are relatively expensive to purchase, but the ribbon and paper are generally much more reasonably-priced than inkjet cartridges, making them far less expensive to operate. The ribbon and paper are normally purchased together as a kit, and normally produce a predetermined number of printouts (300 or 600 per roll).

Sony was once the leader in the dye subliminal photo booth printer arena but the models that were once popular for use in photo booths have been discontinued and it is becoming difficult to find ribbons for them. Nowadays, it seems the new leader it a company called HiTi with their popular 510 series printers. It's worth mentioning, one very nice feature of this printer is its ability to automatically cut 4x6 strip in half, yielding two 2x6 photo strips instantly.

## Photo Inkjet

Inkjet photo printers are extremely common among consumers for household purposes, and they can produce fairly good quality printout; however, they are significantly slower than the dye subliminal printers, and they are not designed for printing large volumes, and the ink cartridges do not last long and are quite expensive to replace. These printers are OK in a pinch or if you are just starting out, but once your volume picks up and you begin operating regularly, you'll notice a long line of patrons standing around waiting for their prints, and will find yourself spending a lot of money on ink. The dye subliminal printers are far superior and well worth the investment.

## Lighting

The word "photo" means light, and you can't have photographs without it. Most weddings and other venues are intentionally dark to create ambiance, and when patrons step inside your booth, it will be even darker. If your camera has a good flash, you may be able to get away without providing any additional lighting, but your patrons will squint when it goes off, and be temporarily blinded by the time the fourth picture is snapped.

Studio photographers employ elaborate and expensive lighting to make their photos phenomenal and some photo booths do attempt to match this level of perfection. However, most booths just provide one or two small supplemental lights either on stands or build into the enclosure.

## Other Accessories

This section lists a few additional accessories common to many photo booths, and provides a brief discussion of each.

## Props

Most photo booth rental companies offer party props either included in their packages or as an add-on item. It may seem silly to some, but most patrons thoroughly enjoy dressing up a little for their photos. Some of the most popular prop items include: sunglasses, feather boas, wigs, Viking helmets, tiaras, crowns, and much more. Props are generally inexpensive, especially if you buy online in bulk, and you can use the same props over again, on average about 3-4 times before they get lost, stolen or destroyed.

## Guestbook

Guestbook's are a very popular add-on, especially at weddings. Normally, the guestbook is setup on a table outside of the booth, and when patrons come out the attendant asks them to paste a copy of their strip into the book and then sign next to their photo.

## Backdrops

The backdrop is what appears behind the patrons in the photos. It can be a curtain, decorated wall, dropdown screen or blue/green screen. The simplest and most versatile backdrop color is solid black. A black background avoids issues with shadows, stains, wrinkles or other unwanted distractions from the people in the photo. However, some customers looking for more excitement and style may desire more intricate backgrounds. This could include intense colors, design patterns, artwork etc.

## Blue/Green Screens

Some photo booth rental companies offer the option to employ a blue/green screen, allowing customers to specify an artificial background such as a city skyline, the ocean or the Grand Canyon. Depending on the photo booth software being used, the background may be preprogrammed by the attendant, or selected by the patrons when they sit down in the booth.

## Decorative Lighting

Some booths employ colored lights, strobe lights or lasers to create an additional excitement or mystique to attract patrons to the booth. This certainly adds additional expense and also increases setup time. However, if you are trying to distinguish yourself from your competition, this is a cool way to set your booth apart from the rest.

## Estimated Total Booth Cost

The table below lists the booth components discussed in this chapter and estimates the low, medium and high costs for each, with totals at the bottom.

|  | Minimum | Average | Maximum |
|---|---|---|---|
| Physical Structure | $100 | $500 | $5500 |
| Camera | $30 | $500 | $1500 |
| Computer System | $200 | $400 | $1600 |
| Software | $60 | $200 | $600 |
| Monitor | $100 | $400 | $1000 |
| Printer | $60 | $1000 | $2000 |
| Lighting | 0 | $150 | $800 |
| Accessories | 0 | $350 | $2000 |
|  | $550 | $3500 | $15000 |

# Chapter 4 – Understanding Your Market

This chapter discusses the first steps in developing your strategy to market your photo booth rental business. These include identifying your territory, conducting market research, evaluating your competition, choosing your niche, and pricing your services. This chapter does not go into detail on developing packages, advertising or sales, as these topics are covered extensively in later chapters.

### Choosing Your Territory

Identifying your territory is a crucial step in developing your marketing strategy. Once you have identified your territory, you can then analyze the local economy to determine the best way to position your services, determine an appropriate price range, and develop advertising campaigns to target the right potential customers.

Most likely, when you start your business, you will focus your efforts on a limited regional territory. After all, you will be required to arrive in person with your photo booth to your client's locations, so for logistical reasons, you should only market your services to an area that is within a reasonable travel distance. There are national photo booth rental companies that market throughout the US, but most of these are either franchise operations with local partners in major cities, or companies that simply subcontract their business to other vendors. For the purposes of this discussion, we'll assume you are starting out small.

The first question you need to ask yourself is: how far are you willing to travel? Do you have a reliable vehicle? Is it worth it to you to drive one hour, two hours, or three hours for a job?

With that in mind, the next question is: where are the customers? If you live in or near a major metropolitan market such as New York, Chicago or Los Angeles, chances are you won't need to travel very far, because you'll be able to find plenty of customers nearby. On the other hand, if you live in a rural area, you may need to cast a wide net around you, and/or identify one or more distant metropolitan areas in which you can commute.

Another factor to determining your territory is your competition. If there are already a lot of photo booth rental companies in your town, you may want to focus your marketing efforts on the next town over.

Once you have an idea of how far you are willing to travel and an understanding of where potential customers are and your nearby competition, pull out a map and mark your territory. It may be as simple as drawing a 100-mile radius around your home base, or you may circle one or more cities or towns.

If you end up with a very large area, you may want to consider expanding your territory in phases. Perhaps start out small in your local town, and then move outward over a period of several weeks or months as you get a feel for how much work you can handle, how strong or weak the market is and how you fair against your competition.

## Get to Know Your Market

Once you know where you are going to market your services, the next step is figuring out what types of customers reside within your territory and what they are looking for. Generally, the most common events for photo booth rentals will be weddings, bar/bat mitzvahs, school dances and proms, private parties (Birthdays, Graduations, etc.),and corporate events.

## Wedding Market

For many photo booth rental companies, weddings are their bread and butter. Wedding customers are year-round, and they are generally more willing to splurge on the higher-priced packages and ask for more add-ons. This is a great market to get into for when you're just starting out.

There are a few ways to familiarize yourself with the local wedding market. First of all, dedicate a few days to Internet searching. Find out where the local wedding venues are and try to determine what type of clients they cater to: are they marketing themselves as an elegant, exclusive venue or as an affordable value reception hall? Also, try to find out their prices. Less expensive places tend to list their prices on their website, whereas high-end venues prefer that you call. You may have to pose as an interested customer and call them to find out.

You should also get to know what other types of wedding vendors operate within your market. This could include: photographers, videographers, DJs, Florists, Limo Services, etc. A great way to do this is to visit wedding vendor directory websites such as theknot.com or weddingwire.com. You may also find local websites that focus specifically on your region. Spent time on these sites browsing each category and get a feel for how many companies are marketing in your territory and survey their pricing and sales bullets. Specifically, hone in on the keywords that they use to describe their services. Are they using words like "elegant" or "premier" or do they use words like "discount" or "affordable". Understanding how other wedding vendors in your area are marketing will give you enormous insight into what your potential customers are looking for, and how you should price your packages.

## Bar/Bat Mitzvah Market

If there is a Jewish population within your territory, then another segment to consider is the Bar / Bat Mitzvah market. Bar / Bat Mitzvahs celebrate coming of age and becoming a full-fledged member of the Jewish community. These celebrations can be huge events, sometimes rivaling the extravagance of a Wedding.

To see if there is a strong Bar / Bat Mitzvah market in your area, you can try performing an Internet search for "bar mitzvah" followed by the name of your city and see how many results come up. You may also visit websites such as partyspace.com or mitzvahwire.com and see how many vendors are listed in your area.

As discussed above for the wedding market, you should survey what other types of vendors are catering to this market, how they are branding themselves, and how they are priced. If you find that there is not a mature market already thriving, you may have to experiment on your own to find out what type of sales pitch and pricing will work.

## School Market
School dances and proms are another popular event for photo booth rentals. The disadvantage of these events is they typically only occur a few times per year, and many schools will have them around the same times. However, on the bright side, there is a great opportunity for repeat business. If you do a good job for a school one year, chances are they invite you back again and again. It may be difficult to find out how other companies are marketing to this market, but it is certainly worth looking into. The first step is to identify high schools and middle schools in your territory, and then attempt to find media outlets in which they participate. Some potential ways to reach them may include the Internet, Social Media websites, or local newspapers. The school may have their own publications as well, such as a school newspaper or yearbook, which may accept advertising from local companies.

## Party Market
This market includes parties such as birthdays, graduations, anniversaries, etc. Although these parties are generally less extravagant than a wedding, they occur much more frequently, and like the school market mentioned above, may lead to repeat business. For example, if you do a good job at a birthday party, they may invite you back for their anniversary. To find out what kind of companies are marketing to these customers, visit event and party planning sites such as partyspace.com or eventwire.com and find out who's listed in your area. You may also search for local event planning websites.

## Corporate Market
The corporate market may be more difficult to break into, as hiring photo booths for corporate events is a relatively new trend, which may not have caught on yet in your area. Still, it is worth pursuing, because these jobs pay well and often lead to repeat

business. You can start by finding out what types of businesses operate in your area. Certain groups such as the pharmaceutical industry or professional trade associations may be more likely to hire you because these businesses frequently host and participate in large events. If there are large venues in your area that specialize in hosting conferences and other corporate events, you may want to contact them to find out what types of events they have scheduled. It wouldn't hurt to ask if they have a preferred vendor list and whether or not they'd be interested in having a photo booth Rental company listed.

## Get to Know Your Competition

In the section above we talk about getting to know the different types of events and customers in your territory, and studying what other vendors are doing. In this section we will focus on getting to know who direct competitors are, and what types of marketing they are doing. Specifically, other photo booth rental companies who operate in the same territory that you have mapped out for your business.

One of the easiest ways to begin is to go to an Internet search engine and type phrases like "photo booth rentals" followed by your city. Scroll through the first three or four pages and you are bound to find the majority of your competitors.

Another thing to do is visit some of the wedding and event websites mentioned above (theknot.com, weddingwire.com, partyspace.com, eventwire.com) and see if there is a category for photo booths listed under your region. If so, visit the websites of companies listed here and see what they're all about.

The important things to look for are:

1. What type of booths do they have?

2. What services do they offer?

3. What is their price range?

4. What is they're sales pitch?

5. Do they have pictures on their website? Of their booth(s), of their events? How do they look?

6. If you were shopping for a photo booth, would you book them? Why or why not?

After you have surveyed your competition, you may want to revisit the map and consider expanding or contracting your territory. If your town already has dozens of photo booths rentals companies, you will likely need to look a bit farther to find customers who haven't already booked with someone else. On the other hand, if you are the first company to setup shop in your region or even if there are only a handful of others, you may find yourself inundated with calls and be unable to meet the demand, in which case you should focus on a smaller area.

## Choosing Your Niche

After you have a clear understanding of the market and your competition, the next step in developing your marketing strategy is to decide on a niche. This will be your specialty, or the key attributes of your business that differentiate you from your competition. If you are marketing to high-end weddings, your niche may be that you're an "elegant" photo booth. You'll need an elegant website, your photo booth should be stylish and sleek, and whoever is operating the booth will need to look sharp. On the other hand, if you are marketing to kid's birthday parties and bar/bat mitzvahs, you may want to brand yourself as the "whacky" photo booth. Use lots of bright colors on your website, show pictures of kids going crazy with all kinds of silly props, and make sure whoever is running the booth shows up with a larger than life personality.

After you have spent time researching your market, and you understand what kind of people live there, what kind of events are going on, and what other vendors are doing, you can brainstorm to come up with ways to differentiate your brand. The best niche is something that can't be easily duplicated. If you can think of any special skill or talent that you have, try to think of ways to incorporate that into the business. Say for example you are artistic, you could paint custom backdrops for the booth, or if you are good at computers, you could design a "high tech" booth. On the other hand, if you can't find anything personal to draw from, there's nothing wrong with borrowing from others. If you find another business that appears to be successful, there's nothing wrong with drawing from their example to take a similar approach. Just make sure to put your own spin on things so they don't accuse you of stealing. Never use the exact same images or phrases, but it's OK to mimic their style and/or use the same type of language.

## Deciding Your Price-Range

There are many different ways to approach branding your business and carving out your niche, but at the most basic level there is a continuum of good vs. cheap. For example, think of the brands Mercedes vs. Hyundai or Saks Fifth Avenue vs. Wal-Mart. There are many nuances to each and cleaver buzz words to describe these opposing ideas, but essentially all marketing leans more towards one or the other.

## Why it Pays to be Good

What's good about being "good" is you get to charge more. If what you're offering is better than your competitors then it makes sense that people should be willing to pay a premium to hire you over them. Naturally, by charging more money for your services, profits will go up, and you can make more money while doing the same amount of work. However, the risk to marketing yourself as superior is that people will have greater expectations of you, and if you fail to deliver then they will be disappointed. This could lead to negative reviews of your business and ultimately damage your reputation.

## Why it Pays to be Cheap

Everybody loves a bargain, and many people are in the habit of price shopping to find the best possible deal. Depending on the economic conditions in your territory, these types of customers may be a minority or the majority. Although, you may not make as much money on a single event, it's possible to generate more business, which could lead to more profits long-term. Another thing to consider is when you are just starting, you may not fully know what you're doing and you may not start out with the best equipment, so honestly you probably will not be "the best" - certainly not as good as you could be. If this is the case, offering your services for a cheaper price may be more appropriate.

One thing to be careful of however, is not to be too cheap, and avoid getting into pricing wars with your competitors. If there are a lot of companies competing at the bottom, there is the potential for the price to get so low that you can't make a profit. If you see this happening in your market, you should strongly consider improving your offerings and rebranding yourself into a higher price-range.

## The Middle Ground

There is nothing wrong with walking the middle road - not too pricy and not too cheap, but just right in the middle. This way you can make slightly higher margins than competing at the bottom, but you don't need to work quite as hard at branding yourself as "the best".

When weighing these options and deciding on a price range you need to consider what other companies in your area are doing. If you are going to compete at the top, you will need to find something that can make you better than everybody else. This could be better equipment, better service, more options, more features, a red carpet, elegance, etc. If you are going to compete at the bottom, make sure your prices aren't so low that you can't make a profit.  If choose somewhere in the middle, you'll have to find the right balance.

# Chapter 5 – Obtaining Your First Booth

This chapter discusses considerations for deciding whether to build or buy your first photo booth, and provides some tips for buying a Booth, as well as a couple sample plans to follow for building from scratch.

## Build vs. Buy

Once you've made the decision to move forward with your photo booth rental business, and you have an idea of your price-range and niche, the next step is to obtain your first booth. You'll have to make a decision whether to build your booth from scratch, purchase a kit or individual components and assemble them yourself, or simply purchase a complete booth already built. There are pros and cons to each, but the decision usually boils down to the type of booth, your budget, and your technical skills and abilities.

The primary advantage to building your own booth from scratch is the cost savings. Buying a pre-built booth can be fairly expensive, whereas you generally can build your own for much less.

Additionally, when you build your own, you have full control over the design and function, and can customize your booth to look and perform exactly as you desire. If you ever decide you want to add a new feature or enhancement to the booth or if something breaks and requires repairs, you'll find it much easier to work on because you designed it and you'll know how everything works.

On the other hand, building your own booth takes a lot time and effort, and requires that have the necessary tools, an adequate workspace to build it in, and a moderate level of technical skills and expertise. If you don't have a lot of spare time, and/or you think building your own booth may be too difficult, then buying may be a better option.

Another issue to factor in your decision is quality. If you are buying a booth that has been professionally designed and manufactured, you can reasonably expect that the booth will look great, and work flawlessly from day one. Otherwise, you would be entitled to a refund. When you build it yourself, the quality will depend entirely on your design skills, craftsmanship, and how much time you are willing to put into it. You'll need to determine how important this is to your business and set a standard for yourself. If you believe you can meet the standard then building your own may be the best way to go. However, if quality is a priority and you have any doubts in your abilities, you may decide it's worth the additional cost to buy.

The chart below summarizes the pros and cons of building versus buying:

|  | Pros | Cons |
|---|---|---|
| Build | - Cost – generally less expensive | - Requires more time and labor |

|  | | |
|---|---|---|
| | • Customized to meet your needs<br>• Easier to enhance and perform maintenance | • Requires technical skills, tools and workspace<br>• Quality may not be as good, may look unprofessional<br>• May require experimenting and troubleshooting to work out bugs |
| Buy | • Requires Less Time and Labor<br>• Requires Less Technical Skills<br>• Higher Quality, more professional<br>• More reliable, less bugs | • More Expensive<br>• Standardized Design<br>• More Difficult to Customize or Repair |

## Questions to ask before Buying a Booth?

If you make the decision to buy rather than build your booth, it is important that you do your homework and perform due diligence before committing your hard-earned money. Purchased booth's can cost anywhere from $5,000-$15,000, which is a lot of money. You'll want to make sure you make the right decisions and don't get stuck with something that's not going to meet all of your needs. Here are some questions to think about when purchasing a pre-constructed photo booth.

### What are the dimensions and how much does it weigh?

Make sure that the size and weight of the booth are manageable. Figure out how you will transport it and where you will store it when not in use. If the booth is large and doesn't break down, you may need either a truck or large van to transport it. Make sure you plan for this ahead of time.

**How long does it take to setup?**
It's important to get an idea of how difficult it is to get the booth up and running. You want to avoid booths that are over-complicated or that take more than an hour to unpack and make operational.

**What equipment is included?**
Find out if the booth comes with everything you need or if there are components that will need to be purchased separately? Specifically, ask if it comes with a camera, printer, computer, monitor, lighting kit, etc.

**Is Software Included?**
Find out whether or not photo booth software is included. If so, find out which product. If it is one of the major photo booth applications, make sure that it has all of the features you are looking for. If it is a customer application developed by the same company who manufactures the booth, try to find out more about it. Ask the vendor to provide you with a list of features, and search online to try to find others who have used it and posted reviews.

**What type of camera does it use?**
If the booth comes with a camera, try to find out what kind it is: DSLR, Point and Shoot, Web Cam, etc. Make sure it consistent with the level of quality that you hope to achieve for your business.

**What type of printer does it use?**
If the booth comes with a printer, find out what kind: Dye

subliminal or ink jet. Again, make sure it consistent with the level of quality that you hope to achieve for your business.

## Can it be customized?
Find out what customizations are available from the vendor, and think about ways you would be able to customize it on your own.

## Does it come with a warrantee?
Find out what type of warrantee is provided b the company. If one of the components has a problem or breaks, will they replace it? If not, will you be able to order replacement parts?

## Is technical support provided?
Find out what type of support is provided by the company. Do they have a phone number? Do they provide email support? What is the turnaround time?

## Building a PVC Pipe Booth
A PVC Booth is probably the easiest and least expensive way to build a booth. The PVC pipes and connectors can be purchased at any home improvement store for somewhere between $50 and $100, and you can use pretty much any type of curtains that you like for an addition $100 to $200. Once you have cut the pipes to the proper lengths and assembled all the right connectors, you should be able to easily put it together and break it down in an hour or less.

On the downside, PVC booth's are not the sturdiest, and may look a bit amateurish and unprofessional. They are also relatively heavy and somewhat bulky when trying to fit into a small car and transporting in and out of the venue. They're an OK choice for just starting out, and are acceptable in the low to mid price range. However, if and when you are willing to spend a little bit more money, the aluminum pipe booth's are usually a slightly better way to go.

Here is a diagram illustrating a typical design for a 4 ft by 6 ft PVC Pipe Booth.

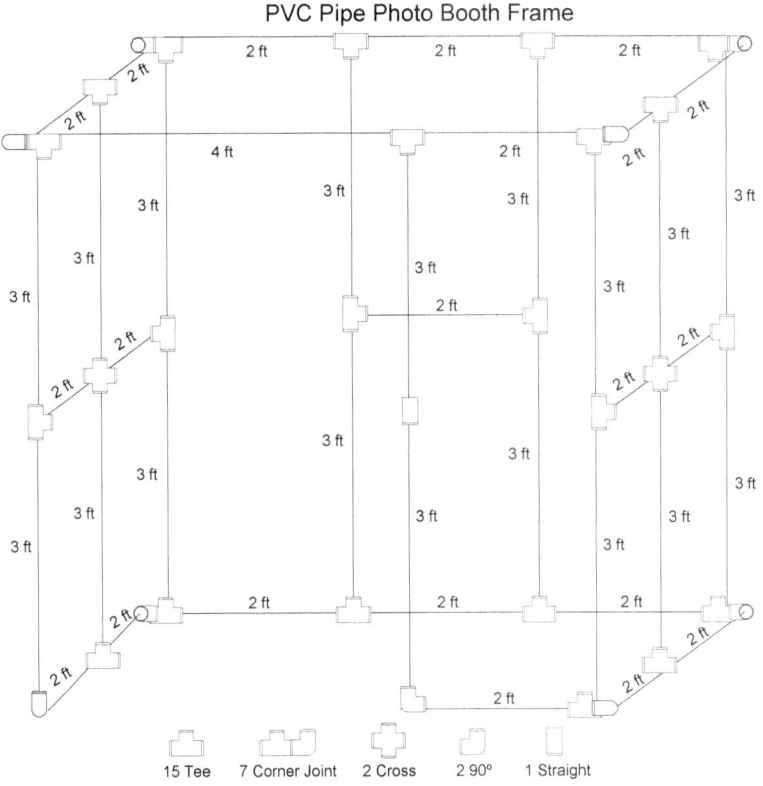

Note: This design is for ¾ inch PVC pipe. The corner joint is made with a Tee connector and a 90 degree connector using a small 1 inch cut of ¾ inch PVC pipe to connect the two together.

## Building an Aluminum Pipe Booth

Aluminum Pipe Booths are slightly more expensive than PVC, but they have the advantages of being sturdier and lighter. They also generally look a bit more professional. Below we demonstrate a simple design using aluminum pipe. You could build this from scratch using ¾ inch aluminum pipe, umbrella stands and PVC connectors purchased from a home improvement store or alternatively using one inch expandable aluminum pipes and bases purchased from an online trade show supply vendor.

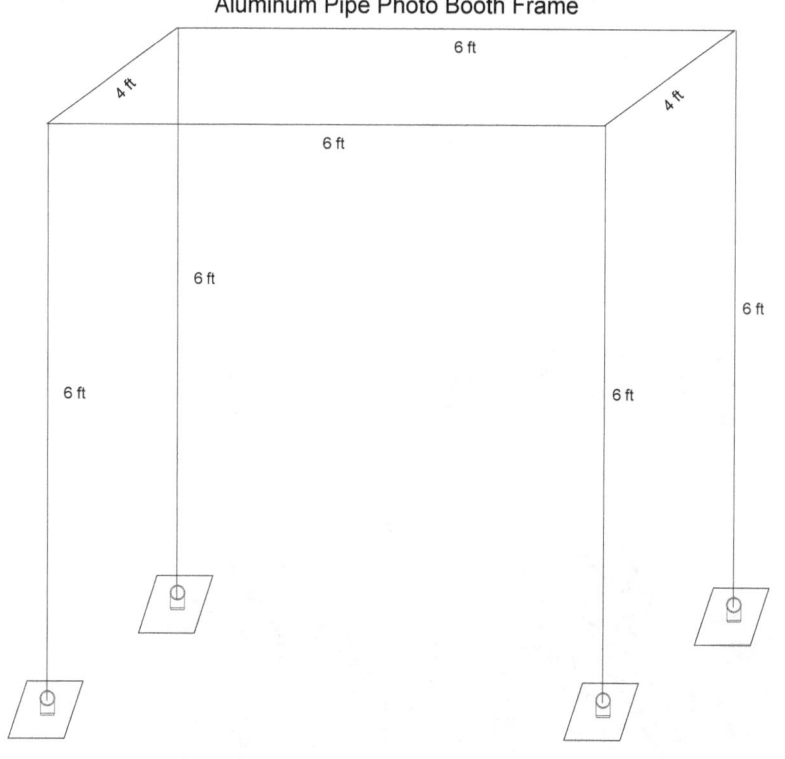

Aluminum Pipe Photo Booth Frame

Expandable Aluminum Poles

Base for Aluminum Poles

## Electronics Enclosures

You may elect to mount your camera, monitor, lighting, laptop, and/or printer in some sort of electronics enclosure. This can improve the presentation and make your booth look more professional, as well as provide protection for your equipment while it is being transported as well as during events. The following photographs show an example of a homemade photo booth electronics enclosure, housing a camera and monitor.

Front view of Electronics Enclosure

Rear view of Electronics Enclosure

## Transporting Your Equipment

It is important to take extreme care when transporting your equipment. Many of the components of your booth (especially the printer and monitor) are not engineered for traveling. Excessive bumping and shaking, being turned upside-down, etc. may damage the internal components over time. In order to protect your investment, and prevent unexpected failures from occurring when you arrive at the event, you should plan on spending some additional time and money on protective carrying cases and wheels to mitigate the stress of travel as much as possible.

### Cases

Everything that's not permanently mounted in an enclosure should be packed into cases during transport. Finding cases for your camera and laptop should be relatively easy, and any standard laptop and camera cases should do. However, your printer and monitor may prove more difficult. The ideal way to transport them is inside a hard case (aluminum or fiberglass) with a foam interior. These cases can be ordered online from companies that specialize in tradeshow gear. They're fairly expensive, usually in the $150-$300 price-range, but they are extremely durable. Alternatively, you may be able locate oversized luggage cases that may work or design/build your own travel cases.

## Carts

Unless your booth is one large unit on wheels, you will likely need a cart to wheel your equipment in and out of venues. The type and size of your cart will depend on the size of your booth and the amount of equipment you need to carry. You may want to look for a large heavy-duty flatbed cart or wagon, or a large canvas folding cart or wagon. You may be able find one at either a warehouse or home improvement store, and you can certainly find them on the Internet from various vendors. Try to find a cart that is big enough to transport all of your equipment in one load, and make sure it is sturdy enough to support the weight. Also, be sure that everything is tied down and secured on the cart using plenty bungee cords in case you hit a bump or need to go up or down an incline.

## Backup Equipment

Obtaining your first booth is a daunting task, and after spending thousands of dollars on such a major investment, it's hard to bring yourself to shell out even more money for extra equipment that you hopefully won't even need. However, it is important to at least have a plan for what you will do in the event that your equipment breaks, either during a job, before or after.

In a perfect world, you would have a duplicate of each piece of equipment on standby in case of a failure. If your printer breaks during a job, you could have someone drop off a replacement within 30 minutes and be back up in running again in no time. This would be ideal. Unfortunately, depending on your budget, this may not be practical when you are just starting out.

You may elect to purchase some lower-end, less expensive equipment for your backups. For example, have a web cam as a backup to a point and shoot camera, or an inkjet printer as a backup to a dye subliminal printer. This way if you have a malfunction, you can still continue to operate until the damaged equipment is either repaired or replaced.

Once your business takes off, and you begin booking fairly regularly, you may want to invest in a duplicate booth. This would give you the option to occasionally double book, running two booths at once, and in the meantime provide you with a redundant set of equipment to serve as your backup. Then, as your business gets bigger, you may even consider having three and four booths.

Another important point, which will be discussed a little later in the book, is to make sure that your contract spells out exactly what the terms are in the event of equipment failure on the job. Normally, your contract should guarantee a specified percentage of uptime, such as 80%, and provide for a pro-rated refund for any downtime in excess of 20%. Contracts will be covered in detail in chapter 7.

# Chapter 6 - Developing Your Packages and Prices

After you have identified your territory, and decided on a price-range and niche, the next thing to do is to develop your packages and prices. This is the breakdown of exactly what services you will offer, and how they are priced. This chapter discusses some of the options you have when structuring your price list, and provides some examples of each.

**Gold, Silver, Bronze**
A very common approach to packaging is to create three levels of service, starting with your most basic offering at the bottom, and then increasing the number of features with each level up. Companies often refer to these packages in terms like Gold, Silver, and Bronze or Basic, Standard, and Premier.

By offering a range of services, you can appeal to customers at various price points. For example, someone on a tight budget may be shopping for something in the price-range of your cheapest package, whereas another customer who is less concerned about cost and wants all the bells and whistles may be happy to pay for your most expensive package. By offering different levels of service you can reach customers at either end of the spectrum.

Here is an example of a Gold, Silver, Bronze pricelist:

## The Bronze Package - $695

- 3 hours Photo Booth Rental
- Photo Booth delivery and removal
- Double Photo Strip Prints
- Onsite Attendant

## The Silver Package - $895

- Photo Booth delivery and removal
- 4 hours Photo Booth Rental
- Double Photo Strip Prints
- Unlimited Photo Strip Reprints
- Onsite Attendant
- Party Prop Box
- DVD with all event Photos

## The Gold Package - $1095

- Photo Booth delivery and removal
- 5 hours Photo Booth Rental
- Double Photo Strip Prints
- Unlimited Photo Strip Reprints

- Onsite Attendant

- Party Prop Box

- Guestbook with copy of all strips

- DVD with all event Photos and Video

- Online Photo Gallery

- Personalized Welcome Screen

- Custom Logo Design on strips

- HD Video messages

## Ala Carte

Another approach to packaging your services is to list each feature you offer and allow your customers to pick and choose. Some customers may prefer this, as it allows them to customize their own packages with all of the features that they want for their event, without having to pay for things that they don't want. The downside to this approach is that it can become complicated, and some indecisive customers may find it difficult choosing which features to include.

Here is an example of an Ala Carte pricelist:

- $295 - Photo Booth delivery and removal

- $100 - Per Hour Photo Booth Rental (includes attendant)

- $50 - Unlimited Photo Strip Reprints

- $75 - Party Prop Box

- $100 - Guestbook with copy of all strips

- $25 - DVD with all event Photos and Video

- $50 - Online Photo Gallery

- $75 - Personalized Welcome Screen

- $100 - Custom Logo Design on strips

- $100 - HD Video messages

## Hourly Rates

Another approach that some photo booth rental companies to take to simplify their pricing, while still appealing to customers with varying budgets is to offer a standard list of features for a flat hourly rate. This way, all customers get the same level of services, it's just a question of how long.

Here is an example of packages based on an hourly rate:

| 2 Hours | 3 Hours | 4 Hours | 5 Hours |
| --- | --- | --- | --- |
| $695 | $895 | $995 | $1095 |

All Packages Include:

- Photo Booth delivery and removal

- Double Photo Strip Prints

- Unlimited Photo Strip Reprints

- Onsite Attendant

- Party Prop Box

- Guestbook with copy of all strips

- DVD with all event Photos and Video

- Online Photo Gallery
- HD Video messages

## Hybrid Packages with Add-Ons

Some companies combine elements from the Gold, Silver, Bronze packages, the ala carte packages and the hourly rate packages to form hybrid packages. For example, you may have Gold, Silver and Bronze packages and three separate hourly rates for each, or have add-ons which customers can choose from, in addition to whichever package they select.

Here's an example of a Hybrid Pricelist:

### The Bronze Package - $195 Per Hour
- Photo Booth delivery and removal
- Double Photo Strip Prints
- Onsite Attendant

### The Silver Package - $295 Per Hour
- Photo Booth delivery and removal
- Double Photo Strip Prints
- Unlimited Photo Strip Reprints
- Onsite Attendant
- Party Prop Box
- DVD with all event Photos

## The Gold Package - $395 Per Hour

- Photo Booth delivery and removal
- Double Photo Strip Prints
- Unlimited Photo Strip Reprints
- Onsite Attendant
- Party Prop Box
- Guestbook with copy of all strips
- DVD with all event Photos and Video
- Online Photo Gallery

## Extra Features

- $100 - HD Video messages
- $100 - Custom Logo Design on strips
- $75 - Personalized Welcome Screen

## Chapter 7 – Contracts

In addition to outlining your packages and prices, it is very important to clearly spell out the terms and conditions of your services. Your customers need to have a clear understanding of what services you will or will not be providing, how and when payments are to be made, who is responsible for what, and what happens if something goes wrong. The best way to do this is by providing your clients with a contract or agreement, and requiring them to sign it in order to book your photo booth.

Many companies today still use printed contracts, although more and more these documents are becoming electronic. Some companies choose to mail or email contracts to their clients and ask them to fill out a hard copy and return it by mail, while others just have them fill it out on their computer and email it back. Another option is to provide the contract on your website, and have clients complete it via an online form. Generally speaking, electronic signatures are legally binding, although some people may not be completely comfortable with this. It's up to you to decide how you wish to handle this for your business, and you may wish to speak with an attorney for advice.

This chapter discusses some of the more common terms, which are often included in photo booth rental agreements, and provides a sample contract. You are free to incorporate any of these terms into your own contract. You may also wish to consult an attorney to make sure your contract is legally enforceable and suitable for your needs.

Disclaimer: This information is not being provided by an attorney and should not be construed as legal advice.

## Business Information

Your contract should clearly identify your business name and contact information. This is normally done in the letterhead at the top of the document. Business information should include:

- The name of your business
- Your business address
- At least one phone number
- Your website address
- An email address
- Fax number (optional)

## Client Information

Your contract should provide an area for your client's name and contact information. This may be a form that they fill out, or a space where you type it in for them. Client Information should include:

- Client's name

- Client's mailing address

- Client's phone number

- Client's alternate phone number (optional)

- Client's email address

**Event Date and Times**

Your contract needs to include the date (or dates) of the event, as well as the rental start and end times. This may be a form that they fill out, or a space where you type it in for them.

**Venue Information**

Your contract should include an area for your client to provide details of the location where the photo booth will be setup. This may be a form that they fill out, or a space where you type it in for them. Venue Information should include:

- Name of venue

- Venue address

- Name of venue contact person

- Venue phone number

**Package and Price Information**

Your contract should include the package or features the client has selected as well as the associated price or prices of each item. The format should be consistent with how your packages are described on your price sheet and/or website. The contract should also include a description of each package or feature detailing exactly what is included.

## Arrival Time

Your contract should make it clear when you plan to arrive at the venue and provide an estimate of how long it will take to setup the photo booth.

## Permission and Accommodations

Your contract should make it clear who is responsible for obtaining permission to operate the photo booth at the venue, and make sure that the venue will make any necessary accommodations. The party who assumes this responsibility is expected to contact the venue and secure their permission to have a photo booth at the event, and make arrangements for where the booth can be setup, making sure that any space and/or power requirements can be met.

## Technical Difficulties

Your contract should state your policy for downtime caused by equipment malfunctions or other technical difficulties. The contract should explain that some downtime for events such as printer jams or minor computer glitches is possible, and should provide a specific figure for acceptable downtime, such as 30 minutes or 15% or rental time. The contract should also explain what will happen if downtime exceeds this. For example, you may offer the customer a partial or pro-rated refund if downtime exceeds the acceptable amount.

## Failure to Comply

Obviously, you are going to do everything in your power to deliver on your promises; however, unexpected things can happen, and there's always a possibility that problems may arise from things outside of your control. Your contract should include a statement that in the event that your company fails to meet the terms of the agreement, that you shall only be liable for funds received. In other words, if you are unable to provide the agreed services, the most that you will have to pay the client is a refund of the money that was paid for your services.

## Liability
You may wish to include a statement indemnifying your business from liability for personal injury or property damages at the event venue. You may need to consult an attorney for advice on how to craft this section and try to get understand what potential liability you may or may not have.

## Copyright
Your contract should state who owns the rights to the photo graphs, which are taken by the photo booth. If you intend to use photographs from the booth on your website or other marketing materials this should be stated.

## Modifications
The contract should state how changes to the agreement are made. Typically, changes to the original agreement must be made in writing and signed by both parties.

## Jurisdiction
The contract should state the legal jurisdiction where the contract shall be enforced. Typically, this is the state where the business is located.

## Cancellation
The contract should explain what to do in the event that either party wishes to cancel the agreement. This should include how a cancellation request should be communicated, deadlines for cancelling the contract and whether a full or partial refund shall be returned to the client.

## Deposits

If you require a deposit, this should be indicated on your contract. The contract should list the deposit amount and when the deposit is due.

## Subtotal/Total Calculation

Your contract should show a breakdown detailing how the total price is calculated. This should include a subtotal of all packages or features selected, a listing of any extras or add-ons, the sales tax amount if applicable, any discounts or reductions, and a grand total representing the total payment amount due from the client.

## Balance Due

The contract should display the total amount of payment due, less any deposits received, and due dates when payments must be received.

## Signatures

The contract should include an area for the client and business representative to date and sign. If you are using an online order form or other electronic document, the signature may be substituted for a text box for the client to type their name.

## Sample Photo Booth Rental Agreement

Below is a sample photo booth rental agreement.

---------------------------------------------------------------------------------------

*Your Photo Booth Company*
*21 Parkside Rd*
*Chicago IL, 60613*
*Phone: 555-555-5555*
*Email: info@photobooth101.com*
*Web Site: www.photobooth101.com*

*Photo Booth Rental Agreement*

# PHOTO BOOTH 101

Client Name: _____
Address: _____
City: _____ State:__ Zip: ____
Email address: _____
Primary Phone: _____
Alternate Phone: _____
Event Date: _____
Rental Start Time: _____
Rental End Time: _____
Name of Venue:_____
Venue Address: _____
City: _____ State:__ Zip: ____
Venue Contact Person: _____
Phone: _____

Selected Package (please check):

| | | |
|---|---|---|
| ☐ | Photo Booth Rental - 2 Hours | $795.00 |
| ☐ | Photo Booth Rental - 3 Hours | $895.00 |
| ☐ | Photo Booth Rental - 4 Hours | $995.00 |

All packages include:

- DVD containing all event photos
- Photo Booth setup and removal
- Onsite technician / attendant
- Use of party prop box
- Unlimited photo strip printouts

Selected Extras:

| | | |
|---|---|---|
| ☐ | Custom Logo/Design | $100.00 |
| ☐ | Scrapbook | $75.00 |
| ☐ | Extra Hour | $100.00 |

*Terms of Agreement:*

1. *Your Photo Booth Company will arrive at event venue approximately one hour before scheduled rental start time to setup equipment and make sure that everything is operational.*

2. *It is the sole responsibility of the client to secure permission of the event venue for Your Photo Booth Company to setup and operate the Photo Booth at this event. The Photo Booth is approximately 5ft by 7ft, and requires access to a 120-volt electrical outlet. The client is responsible to inform Your Photo Booth Company of any restrictions at the site that may affect the setup or operation of the Photo Booth and/or Your Photo Booth Company's ability to adequately perform their duties. The client understands that such restrictions may adversely affect the overall experience and/or quality of photos, and that Your Photo Booth Company is not responsible for the consequences of such restrictions.*

3. *Your Photo Booth Company takes the utmost care regarding equipment function, photo quality, and printing. However, due to the nature of technology, some downtime may occur. Your Photo Booth Company guarantees its equipment to be operational at least 80% of the scheduled rental time, and will refund a pro-rated amount of the rental price for any downtime beyond this caused by equipment malfunction.*

4. *In the event Your Photo Booth Company fails to comply with the terms of this agreement, Your Photo Booth Company will only be liable for funds received.*

5. *Client agrees to indemnify Your Photo Booth Company against any and all liability from any claims, actions, suits, costs, damages or liabilities including but not limited to liability for personal injury of any person at the event, and/or property damage.*

6. *Your Photo Booth Company reserves all rights to the photographs captured during event and may use for demonstration, publication, or other purposes. Original media and copyrights remain the exclusive property of Your Photo Booth Company.*

7. Any individual aspects or particular requests should be made prior to your signing this agreement.

    a. Notes:_____

8. This agreement incorporates the entire understanding of the parties. Any modifications of this agreement must be in writing and signed by both parties.

9. This agreement shall be governed by the law of the state of Illinois.

10. The total price for the above services and product(s) is (package price + state tax 6.25%). Payments shall be due at the following times: 30% initial deposit; the balance is due 10 days before the event date. Payments made before The Event date shall be defined as "Retainer(s)" and are non-refundable upon cancellation of The Event, but may be re-applied subject to availability if The Event is rescheduled. Canceled Events must be rescheduled within 60 days of notice of cancellation in order to re-apply retainer(s).

11. If The Event is canceled, the Client must notify Your Photo Booth Company of his/her desire to cancel the contract, and upon receipt of that information Your Photo Booth Company will provide Client with a cancellation form. This form must be filled out in its entirety and sent to Your Photo Booth Company by certified mail, return receipt. Otherwise, The Client shall be responsible for the payment schedule as set forth above. Rescheduled events shall be subject to standard pricing in effect on the date to which the event has been rescheduled, and any pricing changes shall be documented in a separate addendum.

12. If Your Photo Booth Company cancels the contract due to illness or a non-compliant Client (Client violates any terms of the Contract, Your Photo Booth Company may refund all or a portion of the fees already received. Any fees paid for services/products already completed will not be refunded.

13. A 30% non-refundable deposit is required to reserve your event date. Final payment is due 10 days prior to event.

14. Any failure to make timely payments may result in cancellation of this contract. Your Photo Booth Company will make every attempt to provide notice to Client before cancellation occurs.

*\*\*\*Make all checks payable to: Your Photo Booth Company*

Rental Price: $_____
Extras: $_____
Sub Total: $_____
Tax (6.25%): $_____
Total: $_____
30% Deposit: $ _____
Balance Due: $ _____
Balance Due By: _____

*I have read, understand, and accept the terms of this agreement*

*Client Signature: _____ Date _____*
*Your Signature :_____ Date _____*

---

Note: Please visit www.photobooth101.com to download this contract as a word document.

# Chapter 8 - Designing Your Website

These days, the majority of people use the Internet to shop for products and services and review online information before making a purchase. This is especially true for photo booth rentals. Many customers will perform Internet searches to find a photo booth rental vendor for their event, and others who are referred via word-of-mouth or other methods may not feel comfortable hiring a company without first visiting their website.

If you're like most companies, your website will essentially be your storefront. In many cases, it will be one of the first things your customers see, and will often have a huge influence over whether or not they choose to hire you. This chapter will walk you through the steps of setting up your website, and discuss some of important features you should consider including.

## Domain Name

The first step in created your company's website is registering your domain name. This is the web address that people will type in to access your site. Domain names can be registered online by visiting one of the domain name registrars such as godaddy.com or networksolutions.com. Prices typically range from $5-$15 per year. Many registrars also provide website hosting and offer discounts if you bundle your registration with a hosting plan.

Domain names are registered on a first come first serve basis, so finding a good name that hasn't already been taken by someone else can be difficult. As a general rule, you should try to choose a name that is not too long, easy to remember, easy to spell, and hopefully conveys a message letting people know it's for a photo booth rental company.

When you register your name, you will be given a long list of domain name extensions to choose from. The most common ones are .com, .net, and .org. You can choose any extension that you like, although .com's are generally the most popular, and tend to be the easiest for people to remember.

## Hosting

After you have registered your domain name, the next step is to setup a web hosting account. Web hosts provide website owners with space on their servers to store files and images and make them accessible for users to access online. Hosting is generally charged on a monthly basis and typically will cost about $5-$10 per month.

## Website Design

If you are tech savvy and know HTML and other web programming languages, then you may to decide to design your website from scratch and upload the files onto your web server. On the other hand, if you are not very web savvy or you just don't feel like doing any heavy lifting, there are plenty of services available to quickly develop professional looking websites using online tools to edit content and choosing from various design templates. Some examples of sites that offer quick website builder services include: godaddy.com, networksolutions.com, or squarespace.com.

Whichever route you go to design your site, it had better look good. If customers come to your site and it looks cluttered, or sloppy or just plain lame, they're going to assume that your photo booth is the same, and probably move on to the next company. Also, make sure to check the spelling and grammar throughout your web pages, and proofread your content to make sure it is well-written, easy to understand and gets your message across.

## Packages and Prices

The first thing that visitors to your website will be looking for is your packages and prices. Some companies choose not to list prices, because they would prefer to have customers call to find out, thus giving them an opportunity to sell themselves. The downside to this is many customers won't bother calling and will simply move on to the next company they can find. Whether or not you list your prices, you should at least list what services you provide and explain how things are charged.

## Sample Photos

Your customers will expect to see photos to get a visual sense of what they're paying for. They will want to see pictures of the photo booth itself as well as samples of photos taken by the booth and the photo strip printouts. If you haven't actual taken the photo booth to a venue yet, you'll want to set it up in a well-lit room, preferably without any distracting elements in the background, and take a few photos showing what the booth looks like inside and out. If possible, try to find friends or relatives to pose in the pictures to demonstrate using it, and have them take some silly photos to use as samples. After you actually begin working events, you can replace these pictures with real photos of the booth in action.

## About Us Page

Many people will want to know more about you and your company before deciding to hire you. Your about us page should contain a brief bio of yourself and any of your employees you wish to include, and a brief description of your company. If you are just starting out, you may or may not want your customers to know you haven't been doing this for very long, so you may want to focus on other things, such as where you went to school, how long you have lived in the area, what you interests are, what other lines of work you've been in, etc.

You may also want to include a picture of yourself and/or your employees on the about us page. Many people are weary about online transactions and can be very nervous hiring a company who they know very little about. For some people, seeing a photograph of the person they are dealing with gives them a sense that they're dealing with an actual human being rather than just a website, and can go a long way in easing these concerns.

## Contact

You need to make it easy for people to get in touch with you if they have any questions or are ready to book. You should post your phone number and email address in prominent places throughout the website, and have a Contact page with information on how to get in touch with you. You may also want to implement a contact form, enabling visitors to email you directly from the website. If you are using a website builder service, you will need to check to see if they have this feature available. Otherwise, you may need to do some basic programming to get it to work.

## Online Booking

Some photo booth rental companies have an online calendar displaying their availability and allow customers to book their event online. There are several companies offering online booking applications that can be easily added to your website. This feature can make it easier for customers to be able to book their date without having to talk to anyone. However, depending on how complicated your packages and prices are, and how you decide to handle deposits and payments, this option may be difficult to implement. If you do decide to give it a try be careful that the service is set up properly, and make sure that you stay on top of online reservations.

## Search Engine Optimization

Search engine optimization or SEO is the art of making your website compatible with major search engines in hopes of receiving more visits from people who are searching for your services. When most people use a search engine, they focus their attention of the web pages that appear at the top of the page, and seldom click on links to sites that are ranked below the tenth position or page two of the search results. Therefore, in order to receive significant search engine traffic for a given key word phrase, you will need for your website to appear in the top results.

Accomplishing this is not an easy task by any means. There are entire books dedicated to the topic of SEO, and there are thousands of professionals who do nothing but SEO all day. Depending on how competitive your market is and how much time and money you are willing to dedicate to this, this may or may not be a worthwhile pursuit for you. As discussed later in Chapter 10, there are many other ways to reach potential customers other than search engine results. Nonetheless, there's a high probability that people who are searching for phrases like "photo booth rentals" are good potential customers, so if you can figure out a way to tap in on this traffic you will certainly benefit.

Here are some basic SEO tips to help you get started. This is not a comprehensive list, but just some simple things you can do to try to boost your ranking.

## Descriptive Title and Description

Make sure that each web page has a unique title and description. If you are designing your website on your own, these should be contained within the <title> and <meta> tags within the page header. If you are using a web page builder application you will need to find out where in the application these attributes can be set. Be sure to use the words "photo booth" in both the title and description as well as other keywords such as the primary city where you operate or any special attributes of your business.

## Use keywords in your Page Content

Be sure to work search keywords such as "photo booth" or "photo booth rentals" into the content of your web pages, especially in headings. This will improve the chances that search engines will associate these keywords with your website. However, be careful not to over do it. If you use keywords repeatedly in such a way that wouldn't make sense to your users, you run the risk of search engines identifying your site as spam and ignoring your pages altogether.

## Write a Blog

Blogging is a great way to increase your search engine traffic because every time you write a post, you will be adding valuable content to your site, which search engines can easily crawl and index. Each post will contain unique keyword combinations, which you probably won't even think about at the time, but may result in new traffic as people stumble on your site by searching for similar keyword combinations. Setting up a blog on your website may require some technical skill. If you are using a webpage builder application, check to see if blogging is a supported feature.

**List Your Site in Directories**

Most search engines use backlinks to your web site as a factor when ranking the relevance of your site. Generally speaking, the more links to your web site the better. One effective way to start obtaining links is to list your site in relevant web directories. Some are free, although most of the better ones will require a fee. Listing your site in directories can be expensive, and there is no guarantee you will see tangible results. However, there is no harm in submitting your site to free directories, and if you can afford it, it is worthwhile to list your site in at least a couple paid ones to begin the link-building process.

Here are a few to consider:

Manta – www.manta.com – free business directory

DMOZ – http://www.dmoz.org - free but difficult to get into

Yahoo Directory – http://dir.yahoo.com - $300 per year

BOTW – www.botw.org - $150 per year (or $300 for life)

The Knot – www.theknot.com – price varies by region

Wedding Wire – www.weddingwire.com - price varies by region

**Write a Press Release**

Writing a press release is another good way to generate some initial backlinks to your site. Generally, if you use a newswire service, such as prweb.com or prnewswire.com, your release will appear on several prominent news sites with a link back to your website. Plus, if any local news websites or blogs pick up the story you may receive additional links. Writing a press release will be discussed more in chapter 12.

# Chapter 9 - Selling Your Booth

When potential customers call or email, you will have a short window of opportunity to convince them to book your photo booth. In order to convert these leads into sales, you need to have good communications and a refined sales pitch. You will need to respond to emails quickly, be well prepared when you answer phone calls, follow-up with customers who may be on the fence, and ultimately pull it all together to close the deal.

## Sales Pitch

Your sales pitch is a concise description of what you have to offer and a few compelling arguments for why people should hire you. To begin crafting your message, you need to think about your niche and price-range, and identify the key qualities of your business that will appeal to your audience. You can start by simply writing down a list of things that make your business special or reasons why people should pick your photo booth for their event.

Here are some examples:

- We're dependable, reliable, trustworthy

- We provide free props and unlimited prints
- We use the best equipment, high-end camera, printer and lights

Once you have come up with three of four bullets, start drafting a short paragraph, between three and five sentences long, summarizing these points, and practice reciting it as if you were speaking on the phone. Once you have a good, concise skeleton of what your sales pitch is going to be, you'll be able to adapt it for writing some canned email responses and a phone script.

## Responding to Email Inquiries

The most common way for people to reach out to you will likely be via email. People will usually give you a brief explanation of what they're looking for and ask you if you're available and perhaps ask about packages and prices.

It is absolutely imperative that you respond to these emails right away. The sooner the better, but within 24 hours or less is an absolute must. If you wait longer than this, in most cases by the time they read your email they will have already decided to go with someone else. They may or may not leave a phone number in the email message. If they do, it is your choice whether to call or just email, but it's a good idea to send an email either way in case they forget who they were speaking with or other details of the conversation.

Although every email your type should be custom tailored for the person who sent it, including details and follow-up questions specific to his or her event, you can save yourself a lot of time, and ensure that you don't miss anything, by creating a generic response or template, which can be used over and over again, just by filling in the details for each inquiry.

You should start your email responses by thanking the customer for contacting you. If he or she asked you a specific question, such as "are you available on such and such a date?", then you can also include a quick answer, such as "Good news, we are available for your date" in the first line of the email.

The next thing you should do is ask a few follow-up questions. For example, you could write "Congratulations on your engagement. Where is your reception being held? How many guests are you having?" Psychologically, people are compelled to answer these types of questions, making the urge to respond almost irresistible. This technique is very effective and drawing people in a starting a dialog. Often, by emailing back and forth a few times, people build a sense of trust and will feel more comfortable hiring you.

If you can work it in somehow, you may also want to include a testimony custom tailored for their event. For example, if the event is at a venue where you've worked before, you could write "We just did a wedding there a couple weeks ago. It's a beautiful venue. Everyone always has a fantastic time there." If you have any photos from the event you could attach one or two to the email or send a link if you have them posted online. This may help to convince the customer that you are especially qualified to do their event because you've done something similar before.

After you ask a few questions, and possibly give a testimony, you can then go into your sales pitch, telling them a little bit more about your company and giving them the key reasons why they should pick you. This can either be in paragraph form or bullets. Just make sure it is brief and to the point.

You may or may not want to include a pricelist in the first email response. If your packages and prices are simple, you could include this is the body of your email or if they are more complex you could send it as an attachment, just make sure to mention it in the email. Alternatively, you may find it more effective to wait for them to ask for your prices or give them a call and go over your prices on the phone.

Finally, you should end your email with a call to action. If you feel confident that the customer is ready to book, the call to action could simply be: "Please get back to me soon if you would like book us. It's been a busy month and your calendar is filling up fast." On the other hand, if they have a lot of questions or just seem unsure the call to action could be a request to follow-up: "Please get back to us soon so we can go over the details." The goal is to make it clear and easy for them to understand the next step in the process.

## **Fielding Incoming Phone Calls**

As is the case with emails, it is imperative that you are extremely responsive to incoming phone calls. You should make every effort to answer your phone right away when someone calls, but if you are unavailable and they leave a message, you have to get back to them right away. If you wait more than 24 hours it is generally too late.

If you are not comfortable speaking on the phone, you should take some time to write down a script of things to say, questions to ask and details to go over. You should always start the conversation by asking the customer questions, and be sure to listen carefully and try to let them do most of the talking. Some basic questions are:

- When is the event (make sure you're available)?

- What type of event is it (Wedding, Bar / Bat Mitzvah, Birthday Party, etc.)?

- Where is the event (make sure it is somewhere you are willing to travel)?

- How long is the event?

- How many people will be there?

You may think of salesmen as people have a lot to say, and assume that in order to sell that you need to do a lot of talking. In this case, the opposite is true. Often, the best sales technique is to say very little and encourage the customer to do all of the talking. Ask questions throughout the conversation, and be sure to give them all the time they need to answer. Be mindful not to interrupt them, and listen attentively.

After you get all of the critical information and have given the customer a few minutes of speaking time, now you can launch into your sales pitch. Tell them what your company offers that's unique and why they should hire you, and make it quick, preferably in less than a minute.

Next, begin going over your packages and try to gauge which features or add-ons the customer might be interested in. It's up to you if you want to disclose prices right away or wait for them to ask. Try both approaches and see what works better for you. Again, be sure to pause and give them a chance to speak or ask questions. If you are speaking for more than a minute or two and they don't interrupt you, you should stop and specifically ask them if they have any questions.

Finally, after you have gotten all of their information, given your sales pitch, gone over your packages and answered all of their questions, it's time to close the deal. It's very basic, and yet for many people it's very hard. You simply need to ask them if the want to book. If you don't ask, most customers will not bring it up themselves, and will instead end the call saying something like "OK we'll get back to you". Half the time, they never will. Of course, there is no guarantee that when you ask them to book, that they won't say "no", or "I need more time to think about it", but if you don't ask them, then they probably won't say "yes".

## Follow-ups

You won't always be able to book customers after the first email or phone call. Sometimes you will respond to their email inquiry or call them back and leave a voice mail and never hear from them again. It's important not to just let these leads slip through the cracks and be lost forever. People have hectic lives and it's easy to forget to respond to an email or return a call, and often people are just too busy. This doesn't necessarily mean that they're not interested or that they don't want to book you.

You certainly don't want to pester people, but if you email or call someone and they don't get back to you within two or three days, it's perfectly acceptable to try at least one more time. Some people prefer email and other people are better with phones. If you email twice and still hear no response, you may want to make one last attempt to contact them by phone, or vice versa. After three attempts to contact them, if they still don't get back to you, you can probably assume that either they hired someone else or just changed their mind about having a photo booth. However, don't give up too easily. There are many potential customers out there who just need an extra little nudge before they decide to hire you.

## Deposits/Contracts

After you ask the customer if they want to book, and they say yes, typically their next question is "what do I need to do?" Usually, this consists of two things: a deposit and a contract. Most photo booth rental companies require a deposit in order to reserve a date, and it is a good idea to require the customer to sign your contract at the same time as well. Deposits can range from 10%-30% of the total contract price or could be a fixed amount such as $200 or $300.

The main reason for collecting a deposit is to protect yourself from last minute cancellations. After you have reserved a date, you may have to turn away other customers who inquire about the same day. If the original customer cancels, you will have lost a day's pay, despite the fact there may have been several other customers willing to hire you. It deters the customer from changing their mind about having a photo booth or deciding they want to hire someone else. Plus, in the rare instance that they decide to cancel the event, you at least get to keep the deposit, which is better than nothing.

It's important to get a signed contract from the customer for several reasons. For one thing, it is a good way to collect all of the basic details of the event, in writing, so you'll know all of the what's, where's and when's of the event, and you'll have all of the customer's contact information in case you need to get in touch. Also, the contract should outline the terms and conditions of your agreement. It is much better to get all of this out of the way up front rather than later down the line. This gives the customer an opportunity to raise any objections or negotiate any terms before either one of you has to make any commitments. Refer to chapter 7 for more about contracts.

# Chapter 10 – Advertising

When you first open your doors for business, it will probably be somewhat difficult for potential customers to find you. It can take anywhere from several weeks to several months (or even longer )for search engines to index and rank your website, and you most likely won't receive any word-of-mouth referrals until you've established your company and performed several successful events. In the beginning, you're probably going to need to do at least some advertising to get your name out there, and depending on how quickly things take off, you may decide to continue running ads regularly to keep new business coming in.

In this chapter we discuss several effective online and offline options for advertising your photo booth rental business and some of the pros and cons of each.

## Online

### Wedding and Event Vendor Directories
There are many popular wedding and event planning websites out there, which provide customers with directories of local event

vendors, and often include additional features such as user reviews, price-comparison tools, forums, etc. Some of these websites are free, although most charge vendors a monthly or yearly advertising fee to be included in their directory, and some offer different levels of listings, charging more to be listed at the top of the page or to include more pictures or videos in the description. Listing your company on these sites can benefit your business in several ways.

First of all, many of these sites receive a large number of visitors from people in your area who are in the early stages of planning a wedding or event, and may be in the market for a photo booth. Many of these users will browse through the local vendor directories searching for ideas for their event, and comparing various available services and prices. Depending on how popular the particular website is in your territory and the quality of your listing description, you will almost certainly receive at least some inquiries as a result of this type of advertising. Hopefully, this will at a minimum generate enough sales to cover the cost of the listing.

Another advantage to being listed on these websites is that most of them will provide a hyperlink to your website, which may help with your search engine optimization. As discussed in chapter 8, many search engines count the number of backlinks to your website, and factor this in to their ranking algorithms when determining search results. Listing your website on these sites could give you a significant boost in how often your site comes up when people are searching for photo booths in your area.

Finally, being listed on these websites gives you exposure to a web savvy community. Many of these sites take advantage of social media tools that allow users to share things they find with their friends and post comments on forums and blogs. Even if a particular user on the website isn't interested in a photo booth for his or her own event, maybe that person has a friend who is. Also, if and when you do get hired and you do a good job for these customers, there is a good chance they will go back to the website and give you a positive review.

These websites can be expensive. You definitely need to do your homework on each one before making a decision, and make sure they are used by people in your territory and that they target customers in your price range. There are a few ways to gauge this. For one thing, you could call them and ask and they will probably have statistics on the number of users in your region. You can also perform some Internet searches for "wedding planning" or "event planning" followed by your city and see whether or not these sites come up. Additionally, you can look to see how many other vendors are listed under your region. If there's a lot then chances are the website is relevant to your territory, but if there's only one or two, there's probably a reason for that.

Here are some sites to consider:

www.theknot.com

www.weddingwire.com

www.mywedding.com

## Search Engine Advertising (Pay per Click)
It can be quite difficult to get your website to appear in search engine results; however, most search engines offer the option to advertise your website for a fee. This is generally charged on a pay-per-click basis, meaning that you bid on keywords that you believe are relevant to your business, and every time someone

clicks on your ad your account will be charged. The price you pay per click will depend on how many other advertisers are also bidding on the same keywords. If you are the only company bidding a specific keyword phrase, the price per click may be as low as $.05, but if there are hundreds of bidders, often the price get driven up as high as $2.00-$3.00.

Search engine advertising is effective because it is highly targeted. Your ad will be shown to people who are actively searching for your services. However, if you are doing business in a highly competitive territory, the costs can potentially exceed your profits.

It's a good idea to give search engine advertising a try, and experiment with different keywords to see how much they go for in your market, and how effective these ads are in landing you sales. If you search the web, you may be able to find coupons for free advertising credits to give these a try with no risk. However, be cautious that you don't end up spending more money on the ads than you back in sales.

Here are some search engines offering PPC advertising:

www.google.com

www.bing.com

www.yahoo.com (powered by Bing)

## Social Media
Social Media websites are a great way to advertise your business, and the best part is that most of these services allow you to create business profiles for free. What makes these sites so powerful is they allow users to share things with hundreds of

people instantly, who in turn can spread the message to their friends and in no time at all thousands or even millions of people are engaged. Most of these sites are free and only take a few minutes to setup. There is no excuse not to take advantage of these. Once you have created your accounts and profiles, try to think of ways to integrate them into your business.

The most obvious thing to do is to post photos from your photo booth online. You may want to ask you permission first, especially if the event is for children, but most people will be OK with this. You can let people know how to find the pictures either by emailing your customers with a link or handing out cards at the event. Some companies also place a sticker on the back of the photo strips after they get printed with a link to an online photo gallery. Once a few people at the event start clicking through and sharing the pictures, quickly their friends and family will begin doing the same. This can give your company exposure to hundreds or even thousands of new potential customers, and it doesn't cost you anything.

Here are some social networking sites you should definitely consider:

FaceBook - www.facebook.com

Twitter - www.twitter.com

Google Plus - http://plus.google.com/

## Coupon Sites

Coupon websites are very popular these days among small businesses. These sites enable companies to advertise promotions to large numbers of people. This can be an effective way to kick start a new photo booth rental business by booking dozens of customers within the first couple days; however, before committing yourself to one of these programs, make sure to take a careful look at the terms and conditions.

These programs require you to offer your services at a significantly reduced price, and often they will take up to 50% of the money. This makes it very difficult to make any profit, and in fact you may end up taking a loss. Make sure you are willing and able to deliver on however many contracts you sign during the promotion, and make sure it is worth it to you. This can be a good way to get your name out and get your business off the ground quickly, but it comes with a steep price, and it may not be worth it if you end up operating at a loss.

## Offline

### Bridal and Event Magazines

There are many bridal and event magazines which offer advertising opportunities for local vendors. This form of advertising can be moderately effective, although the circulation and advertising costs of these publications vary a lot per region. It is worthwhile to look into this as an option; however, this will probably not be your primary advertising method.

### Direct Mail

Occasionally, photo booth rentals companies use direct mail to send brochures or coupons to potential customers. You may be able to obtain targeted lists from bridal boutiques or local marketing companies, and design and printout mailers yourself or pay for a marketing company to do this for you. This form of advertising tends to be a little bit expensive and may or may not be cost effective. You may be able to convert perhaps one out of hundred of these mailers into a sale, but the costs of printing and postage make this a questionable approach.

## Bridal Expos

If you are operating within a major metropolitan area, there probably will be at least a few major bridal expos in your market each year. Setting up a booth at these events can be a very effective way to find new customers. You'll have the opportunity to speak with dozens of potential brides and demonstrate your photo booth for them live and in person. Many of these brides may not have previously considered having a photo booth at their wedding but if they see yours up close they may decide they just have to have one. Renting a space at these expos is expensive, but if you are able to book even just a few weddings it will be worth it.

## Word of Mouth

Word of mouth is the best form of advertising because it doesn't cost you anything and people are much more likely to hire someone if they have a personal reference. Of course, you won't receive very many word of mouth referrals in the beginning until you start doing a lot of events, but it is important to always deliver on your promises, maintain a professional appearance, and be willing to go the extra mile to keep your customers happy. If you consistently do good work, people will appreciate it and refer you to their friends and family.

## Partnering With other Vendors

When you work events you will come across various other event vendors such as photographers, videographers, DJs, caterers, floweriest, etc. As you get to know other vendors in your area, it's a good idea to try to work out strategic partnerships, whereby you refer business to them and they return the favor. Sometimes this is done just as a courtesy, and other times different companies pay each other finder's fees such as 10%-20% of the sale. This can be done informally based on a handshake or you may want to actually enter into a contract or revenue sharing agreement. This is a great way to obtain new customers by having other vendors make the sale for you.

# Chapter 11 - Event Preparations

This chapter discusses things that need to be taken care of before an event to make sure that you arrive on-time, have everything you need, and are able to setup, operate, and breakdown the photo booth without a hitch.

## Review the Contract

It is very important to carefully review each contract before the event. Often you will be booking events weeks or months in advance. Once you begin booking dozens of jobs, it will become very difficult to remember the details of each. Preferably, you should get into the habit of reviewing your contracts a day or two before the event, and plan on taking one last look at it the day of the event, to make sure that you have all of the details correct.

Here is a list of important details to confirm:

- Verify the correct address of the Event
- Verify the start and end times

- Review selected packages and add-ons

- Review any special requests

- Verify all payments have been received or arrangements have been made

## Schedule Travel and Setup Time

Make sure to map out directions to the event and determine how much travel time is required. It is a good idea to plan for potential traffic jams or other delays, and allow at least an extra 15-30 minutes on top of whatever the normal travel time would be. If you don't already own a GPS, this may be a good investment. If you are ever get lost travelling to an event in an unfamiliar town, a GPS can come in extremely handy.

You also need to consider how long it will take to transport your equipment into the venue and set it up. Every venue has their own procedures for outside vendors coming in. Some will let you walk in through the front door, while others will require you to use the loading dock. If the venue is a large hotel, often you will be asked to use a freight elevator, which can be very slow. Additionally, when you arrive at the venue they may or may not have a designated space already setup for you, you may have to wait for them to clear a space for you, and you may have to run an extension cord.

If you are working at a venue for the first time, you may want to call ahead and discuss logistical arrangements with them in advance. Be sure to allot yourself enough time to figure out where you're going to setup, transport all of your equipment into the facility, and get the photo booth up and running. Generally, you should assume this will take at least one hour, and if you are unsure about the location, possibly allow even more.

You don't want to be rushing, and you don't want to be late. When estimating how much time everything will take, and scheduling out the day, it's always better to error on the side of caution. Once you've been in business for several months and are more comfortable with the procedures, you can relax this to point, but when you're first starting out, it is essential to plan ahead and give yourself plenty of extra time to deal with unexpected complications.

## Equipment Testing

It's a good idea to perform routine tests of your equipment before an event. Here are some things to check:

- Make sure that everything powers on.

- Make sure that your computer is patched and up-to-date. You don't want to turn it on at the event and discover that updates must be installed before it will boot.

- Test your printer by printing a test page. See your printer's manual for other routine maintenance tips, cleaning, etc.

- Make sure that everything is clean and not damaged.

- If you are using curtains, make sure they aren't wrinkled or stained.

## Things to Bring

In addition to the obvious stuff like the Camera or the Printer, there are a lot of little things that you might not think of, which can come in very handy at events, especially when something unexpected occurs. Here are some examples:

- Extension Cord – It should be specified in you contract in advance that the venue must supply you with a 120V three-pronged receptacle, but it's not uncommon to arrive at an event and find out that the receptacle is 25 ft away from where they want the booth to be setup. You should always bring an extension cord to the event, and should be at least 25ft, ideally 50ft.

- Power Strip / Surge Protector – Always bring your own power strip / surge protector with enough outlets to power all of your devices.

- Gaffers Tape – Should always be used when running an extension cord or any cables across where people may be walking.

- Duct Tape – Possibly, the most useful tool in world - comes in handy for all kinds of emergency repairs to the booth or equipment.

- Hammer, Screw Drivers, Scissors – In case you need to make emergency repairs.

- Small Flashlight – comes in handy when trying to work in a dark room or when looking for small items that may get lost.

- Folding Table, Folding Chairs – Depending on the venue, tables and/or chairs may or may not be provided. If you're unsure, it's a good idea to bring a small folding table of your own and at least two folding chairs.

- Bottled Water – It's a good idea to keep hydrated while you're working, and you can't assume you'll be offered a drink at the event.

- Pen and Paper – in case you need to write down special instructions, a phone number, etc.

- Small dust pan and broom – It's a good idea to cleanup any trash and debris from your props after you break down. Leaving the space a little cleaner than when you got there is good way to impress the venue and possibly have them refer you for future events. Leaving a mess behind may irritate the staff, and could possibly lead to having your business banned.

- Business Cards – Lots of people will come up to you at the event and ask you for a card. This is a great way to get new business.

- Copy of the Contract – You should always bring a copy of the contract with you to the event. You can use this as a reference in case your forget any of the details of the event or in case you need a phone number to get in touch with the client or the venue. You may also need to pull it out in case there is any dispute between you and the client as to what was agreed to (i.e. start time, end time, add-ons, etc.).

## Going over the Checklist

It's important to take an inventory of all of your equipment and accessories and make yourself a checklist of everything that is needed to operate your photo booth. You should always go over the check list the day of the vent and verify that you have packed everything you will need. Here are some common items to include:

- All of your major components
    - Physical structure (The Booth, Pipes, Curtains, Backdrop, etc.)
    - Camera
    - Computer
    - Monitor
    - Printer
    - Lights
    - Accessories
- Cables
    - Power Cables
    - USB Cables
    - Monitor Cable(s)
    - Extension Cord
- Extra Printer Ribbons or Ink Cartridges and Paper
- Props
- Tools
    - Rubber Mallet
    - Screwdrivers

- - - Scissors
  - Flashlight
  - Dust Pan and Broom
- Supplies
  - Duct Tape
  - Gaffers Tape
  - Pen and Paper
- Folding Table / Chairs
- Bottled Water
- Directions
- Business Cards
- Contract

# Chapter 12 - Launching

The big day has finally come. You have formed your company, done your research, obtained your booth, developed your packages and prices, designed your website, and are ready to begin doing business. This chapter discusses the final steps to turning the key and launching your photo booth rental business.

## Planning a Dry Run

It is highly recommended that you perform at least one dry run with your booth before taking it on a paid job. You need to make sure that everything works and there are no bugs, and also that you are completely comfortable setting it up, running it, and breaking it down. The last thing you need is to show up to a real event and encounter embarrassing problems. This can damage your company's reputation and if you end up issuing a refund, you won't make any money anyway.

If you have a friend or relative who is getting married or having a large party, this would be a perfect opportunity to try it out. Ask them if you can setup your booth and let the guests test everything out for you for free. Make sure to do everything as if you were going on a paid job: bring all of your equipment, props, guestbook, etc.

If you don't know anyone who is having an upcoming party, try to find a nearby event that might let you setup the booth for free. This could be a charity event, a beef and beer fundraiser, a school or community group function, etc. Search the Internet or your local newspaper and try to find such an event and then simply call them and tell them you would like to donate your photo booth as a way to help make the event a success. Not only is this a good opportunity to test everything out, but it will also give your company some great exposure to the community, and may lead to some early word of mouth referrals.

At the end of the night after you have completed your first dry run, sit down and make a list of lessons learned. Write down everything that worked well, and any mishaps or things that went wrong during the event – there are bound to be a few. Next, come up with strategies to overcome these problems. Hopefully, most will be simple fixes; however, you may find that there are critical deficiencies in the booth or in your process that need some serious attention. If this turns out to be the case, you'll thank yourself for catching these before going live.

After completing a dry run, you'll know whether or not you're ready. If everything went relatively smoothly and everyone had a great time then you should be good to go. On the other hand, if you find some major issues or flaws, you may want to spend some time working things out and try again with a second or third practice job before booking any paid events. A few setbacks can be frustrating, but don't give up, and remember it will be well worth it once you go prime time.

## Press Release

When you are ready to officially launch your business, you may want to consider writing a press release and submitting it to an online press release distribution service. This serves several important functions to help get your business off the ground.

First of all, it is a great way of announcing your new business to the world. Your press release can explain what type of business you are, what services you offer, and what makes you special. If you are lucky, someone from a local media publication or blog will pick up the story, giving you invaluable free advertising and exposure to your community.

Additionally, your press release will be distributed to hundreds of online news sites automatically, generating hundreds of high quality backlinks to your website. These links will dramatically improve your search engine ranking. Within several weeks, you can expect to see a significant boost in your website's position within relevant search results.

Finally, publishing a press release can make your business appear to be more legitimate and professional. Many customers are hesitant to hire companies they've never heard of before, and will want to do some research on your company before they sign a contract. If they perform a search on your company and find articles about you in legitimate news outlets, it will go a long way to convince them that you are not just a fly-by-night startup, but rather you are serious about your business.

There are several options for distributing your press release. Most charge a fee between $100-$300, although some are free or very cheap. Generally, you get what you pay for. The paid services will distribute your release to more major news sites and will result in more exposure and more high quality backlinks. On the other hand, if paying for one of the more expensive options is outside of your budget, submitting to a free or inexpensive service is certainly better than nothing, and will yield you at least some if not all of the benefits discussed above.

Here are some options for online press release distribution services:

- PR Web – www.prweb.com
- PR Newswire – www.prnewswire.com
- PR Log – www.prlog.org
- 24 by 7 Press Release - www.24-7pressrelease.com

## Advertising Campaign

As discussed in chapter 10, you should plan on doing some advertising early on once your business is launched to start generating some initial leads to get started. Once you have evaluated all of the different advertising options, you should decide on one or two primary methods to focus on and begin designing your campaign.

## Copywriting

You will need to write some concise, easy to follow, and catchy ad copy to explain what it is that you're advertising and entice potential customers to take further action either by clicking on the ad to visit your websites, emailing, or calling. There are many different types of ads, and channels to distribute your message, but many of them have the same basic attributes.

- **Headline** – many ad formats require some type of headline. Headline's are usually just a few words or a short sentence that captures the essence of what you are advertising. It could be just the name of your business such as "Your Photo Booth Company" or something basic like: "Chicago Photo Booth Rentals". If price is key to your campaign, you may want to include it here: "Photo Booth Rentals only $595". On the other hand, if you have a strong niche you want to convey try to work it in: "Elegant Photo Booths". Make sure your headline is short, to the point, and expresses the core of what your business is all about.

- **Description** – many ad formats require a description. This can vary from one to three sentences to one to three short paragraphs. In either case, you need to identify your three to four top bullet items that differentiate your business and sum them up here. Explain what you offer, frame it in the context of your niche, word it using the language of your target audience.
- **Photographs** – many ad formats require photographs. This can be anywhere from one images to a gallery of many. If you have a good looking booth and can produce some professional quality stills of it then include this here. If not, then use samples images of people inside the booth having an amazing time.

## Measuring Results

When you run an ad, it is important to keep a close eye on results. Find out how many visits your website receives after running the ad, how many emails and calls do your receive and ultimately, how many events do you book. You can use these statistics to determine how effective your advertising campaign is, how much it costs in terms of ad dollars to book an event, and how much advertising you will need to sustain and grow the business.

Once you establish a method for tracking results, you can experiment by making small tweaks to your campaign and determining if the changes make things better or worse. Try using different headlines, descriptions, pictures, etc. Just be careful not to make too many changes as once, as this will make it difficult to know for sure which changes caused the observed effect. Instead, make your changes gradually, only changing one thing at a time, and be sure to wait long enough to measure reliable results.

# Chapter 13 - Managing Your Business

Once your business is up and running, you have regular bookings, and money is coming in and out, it is important that you dedicate some effort to properly managing your business.

## Accounting

Accounting is important for two reasons. First of all it is required by the IRS as well as your state and local tax authorities, in order to report how much money your business makes for tax collection purposes. Secondly, it is important for you understand how much profit your business is generating to be sure that you're doing things efficiently. If profits are not as good as they should be, you probably need to cut costs or raise prices. The only way to identify this is with good accounting.

You'll need to decide whether to do your own books or to hire a professional. Accounting is generally not rocket science, and there are many good software products to assist you; however, it can be time-consuming to keep with entering all of your invoices into your accounting system, and this requires a great deal of discipline. If you are terrible at math or you just don't think you'll have time to stay on top of it, then try to find a reasonable accountant in your area to work with. Otherwise, make sure to find a good accounting program that you feel comfortable using and dedicate a few hours every week for bookkeeping.

Here are a few accounting software choices:

- Intuit QuickBooks
- Sage Peachtree
- AccountEdge

## Employees

As your photo booth rental business grows you may decide to take on some helpers. You may decide you need an extra hand transporting your booth, setting it up, and running it, and eventually, you may decide to expand and have multiple booths, working at several events simultaneously. You'll have to decide how you want to pay these people, whether you want to pay them in cash, as independent contractors or as part-time or full-time employees.

Paying workers in cash "under the table" is generally frowned upon. Employers are required to pay payroll tax and workers compensation insurance for their employees and bypassing these obligations is technically illegal. Nonetheless, the fact of the matter is many companies do choose this approach, especially when the workers are only working a few hours here and there. It is certainly much easier to simply hand them cash at the end of the night rather than filling out a bunch of paperwork, and some people would prefer to be paid in cash to avoid paying taxes and other deductions.

If you choose to pay workers under the table, be advised that besides being illegal, there are several risks and disadvantages associated with doing this. Your accounting and other financial management reports will not paint a clear picture of what's going in with your finances, as a major cost of doing business is not being reported. Also, your workers will not be eligible for unemployment compensation and will not be building their social security benefits. Finally, if your workers ever have an accident or are injured on the job, you will not be protected by workers compensation laws and you and/or your company may be liable to pay for medical bills and other damages.

Another option for paying your workers is to classify them as independent contractors. This approach has the advantages of requiring less paperwork, and avoiding having to pay payroll taxes or workers compensation insurance; however, this shifts much of the burden from the company to the worker. Your workers will become responsible for paying their own taxes. Workers will need to complete a W9, and at the end of the year you will need to give them a 1099-MISC reporting the total amount they were paid. The IRS does have guidelines for differentiating an employee from an independent contractor. If you do decide to go with this option it is important to research this further and make sure you utilize your independent contractors appropriately.

Of course, if you are serious about expanding your business, and will be relying heavily on regular assistance from others, the best approach is to make them employees. The IRS and the Small Business Administration have several resources available to assist you with hiring employees. Your employees will need to complete a W4 and you will be required to complete a W2. Your state will have additional reporting requirements as well.

Here are some websites to help you navigate the process:

http://www.sba.gov/content/10-steps-hiring-your-first-employee

www.irs.gov

## Finances

As you operate your business and grow, you will need to manage your cash flow and finances. You will have various ongoing expenses including advertising, printing supplies, equipment maintenance, transportation, etc. and as you expand you will need to purchase additional equipment and possibly pay employees or contractors. It's important to have a plan for how you will manage these costs and be prepared for unexpected expenses, for example if a major piece of equipment is damaged and needs to be replaced. Here are some options for financing business expenditures:

- **Cash** – If you start out with a large amount of cash and your business's cash flow continues to be strong you may be able to operate your business without taking on debt. This simplifies things significantly and avoids interest expenses and other financing charges, but may not be realistic for most businesses.
- **Credit Cards** – You may elect to use personal credit cards and/or apply for a business credit card in order to purchase supplies and equipment and pay for business expenses. Credit cards are convenient, offer some protection in case of fraud or damaged merchandise, and may offer cash back benefits and other rewards. However, credit cards typically come with very high interest charges and other fees, especially if you do not pay off your balance within 30 days. It's a good idea to have credit cards available and use them responsibly, but they are not ideal for financing large purchases, and should not be used in situations where you will not be able to pay off the balance within 90 days.

- **Business Loans** – You may qualify for a business loan or a line of credit from a bank. These loans are more difficult to acquire than a credit card and may be harder to qualify for, but they generally come with much better interest rates. If you are financing a large purchase that you do not plan to repay within 90 days, this is probably a better option than using a credit card.

# Chapter 14 - Customer Service

It is extremely important to keep your customers happy. Happy customers may become repeat customers, and will refer you to their friends and family. Unhappy customers can damage your reputation and potentially put you out of business. This chapter discusses some tips to keep your customers happy, and quickly resolve issues if they arise.

## Professional Communications

The key to providing good customer service is to strive for good communications. Your customers should have a clear understanding of what services you will provide, and more importantly you need to understand what your customers are asking of you.

When you're trying to communicate information, keep it simple and to the point. Avoid using language that is overly technical or bombastic. Chances are doing so won't impress people, it will just confuse them. It is important to be honest and forthcoming about what you have to offer and any limitations you may have. It is much better to be upfront about these things and get them out of the way beforehand rather than have to explain yourself to an angry customer afterwards.

Your written publications such as your website, brochures, pricelists and contracts should be well-written, logical and refined. Be sure to spell-check, grammar check, and proofread everything before publishing. Make sure that all important information is included and explained where appropriate. Make sure that your information is accurate, and up-to-date. Your website and other publications should be reviewed at least one per month to make sure that everything is still applicable.

When writing emails to customers make sure to take a little extra time to ensure everything is correct before you hit send. Avoid using slang or texting language. This can lead to confusion, especially if the emails are read out of context. Make sure to spell-check, grammar check and give it a quick read when you're done typing. Never use sarcasm in an email because it generally does not make sense in written form. Keep in mind, that unlike phone conversations, emails are permanent. Off-hand comments or remarks will not be simply forgotten, so make sure you never say anything you might someday regret.

When speaking on the phone or in person with a customer, remember to listen carefully, and never interrupt. If you don't understand something the customer says, ask them to explain. Speak slowly and clearly and again don't try to impress them with your command of technical jargon or vocabulary. It's much more important that you get the important information across so that it is clear and they understand. If you get the sense that they don't get something, pause for a second and ask them if they understand everything so far or if they have any questions.

Finally, if you call a customer and receive a voice mailbox, always leave a detailed message. It is very unprofessional to just hang-up. Considering that most people have caller id on their phones, they'll know it was you who was calling. Always give them your name, the name of your company, your phone number and the reason why you called.

## Avoiding Misunderstandings

As discussed above it is important to have good communications and make sure that your customer understands what you are offering, and that you understand what the customer wants from you. The key to avoiding misunderstanding is to manage your customer's expectations. If the customer expects you to deliver the world, and you fall short in some way, they are going to be disappointed.

Never make promises you can't keep, and further, never allow your customer to believe you will be giving them something beyond what you're capable of delivering. You need to be upfront about what is included and what isn't and never agree to anything out of the ordinary unless you are absolutely sure you can do it.

Make sure that everything is in writing. First of all, everything that you have agreed to provide should be spelled out in your contract, and signed by both parties. If the customer has made any special requests they should be written in and initialed. Your contract should also spell out your terms and conditions and outline the responsibilities of both parties (see chapter 7). Additionally, any discussions that go over details beyond what is covered in the contract should be documented in an email. Even if these conversations take place over the phone, you should take notes and summarize the phone call in an email to the client. This provides proof that the conversation took place, and gives the customer an opportunity to respond in case there was something that you missed or misunderstood.

## Dealing with an Unhappy Customer

From time to time, no matter how hard you try, sooner or later you are going to encounter an unhappy customer. There are some people who simply can never be satisfied, and there are certain things that can happen that are outside of your control. It's just an unfortunate reality of doing business. Here are some things you can do to try to assuage the situation and hopefully prevent the customer from retaliating.

First of all, always remain calm and polite when dealing with angry customers. Never loose your temper and bite your tongue when you feel the urge to say something discourteous. Listen carefully to what they are saying and nod your head. Whether or not you agree with what they are saying, it is important that you at least acknowledge that you understand their point of view on the matter.

If the problem is something that is your fault, take responsibility. Apologize to the customer and offer them a remedy to make up for it. If you started late or if the booth was down for an extended amount of time, offer to stay later or refund a portion of their money back to them. If the event was a complete disaster and you didn't deliver at all, give them a full refund.

If the issue is a misunderstanding regarding what was agreed to, pull out the contract and go over it with them, politely explaining where the communications breakdown may have occurred. Try to find a solution that will make them feel better about it, even if it requires making a small concession, such as staying late, or offering a small partial refund. You can also try simply asking them if there is anything you can do to make it right. If it's within reason, try to comply.

Some people are just plain impossible, and you may find yourself in a lose-lose situation, but if you strive for good communications, manage your customers expectations and are earnest when it comes to resolving problems, ninety-nine percent of the time you'll end up with a happy customer.

# Chapter 15 - Expanding Your Business

Once you have established a successful business, it is natural to want to expand it. After all, at this point you have proven yourself capable. Whatever you are doing is working, so why not take it to the next level. This last chapter discusses three ways to expand your business: obtaining additional booths and operating them simultaneously, widening your territory into new geographic regions, and exploring new services to offer in addition to photo booths.

## Multiple Booths

When you get to the point that your calendar is full, and you find yourself turning away customers, it's time to think about getting more booths. Having multiple booths makes it possible to book two, three or even more events at the same time. Obviously, you will not be able to deliver and operate all of these booths yourself which means you will need to find reliable people to help.

It's important to recruit associates who are bright, outgoing, resourceful and most importantly trustworthy. Remember, these people will be representing you and your business. If they are late, rude, or incompetent this will reflect very badly on your good name and will quickly tarnish your reputation. Once you find a good worker, make sure they are adequately trained. Spend at least a few hours going over everything with them showing them how everything works, and take them with you on at least three or four jobs before letting them go out by themselves. Make sure to pay your employees fairly, and treat them well, and most of the time they will return the favor with loyal service.

Be careful not to expand too quickly. Try out two booths for at least a few months before jumping to three, and then try three a while before going to four. If you take on too much all out once things quickly become unmanageable and you are bound to get yourself into trouble, missing events, having equipment failures, etc. Take it slow and keep close tabs on your employees to make sure they are performing to your expectations. Follow-up with your customers after events to make sure they were completely satisfied with your employee's work. If at any point you start to notice the quality is slipping, it's time to slow down, retrain and get things back under tighter control.

## Expanding Your Territory

If you feel that you have reached your peak for the amount of business you can acquire in your current territory, and you're looking for a way to increase your revenue, expanding your territory is a good option. You may approach this by simply expanding the radius around your home base where you advertise, or you may begin targeting remote cities, perhaps as far as an hour or two away.

Make sure you that you set realistic limits for how far you are willing to go, and make sure that your vehicle is in good enough condition to make frequent long distance trips. You certainly don't want to break down on the way to a job.

Also, be sure to factor in your travel expenses when determining your prices, and make sure that the additional costs don't exceed your profit margin. A good number to use when calculating your driving expense is $.50 per mile. If you have to drive 100 miles to get to a job, your travel expense for that trip would be $100 (100 miles both ways times $.50). If this cuts too deep into your profit, you may want to raise your prices.

Also, make sure that the extra commuting doesn't interfere with the business you already have at home. For example, it's not uncommon to book two events in one day on Saturdays - one in the afternoon and one at night. However, if you have to drive two or three hours to a far away job on a Saturday afternoon, you might not be able to make it back in time for a second job that night. If you find this type on conflicting occurring often, you might want to think twice before booking jobs out of town.

## Offering Additional Services

Once you have perfected the art of selling your services and you have learned the ins and outs of working weddings and event venues, you may consider utilizing those skills to offer other types of similar services.

In addition to photo booths, there are lots of other party rental items such as karaoke machines, video projectors, chocolate fountains, popcorn machines, tents, tables, chairs, and more, which are popular among the same customers who hire photo booths. If they're going to have these items at the same party where you're hired to set up a photo booth, why not offer to supply some of the other stuff too? Of course you will need to do your homework, and learn everything there is to know about these other offerings before jumping in, but it's something to consider when you're thinking of ways to increase sales and broaden your services.

Another great business to look into is event photography. Photographers are an absolute must-have at weddings and other large events, and many of them make a good living. You will need to make a significant investment in professional cameras and equipment, and should probably take a course in photography and perhaps shadow a professional photographer for some time before officially crossing over. But many of the same skills that are required to operate a photo booth rental business can be easily applied to running a photography business.

You might also consider exploring a business providing event videography. Like photography, this will require a substantial investment, and several months of practice and training, but if you are looking for a good way to add a new revenue stream to your business this may be a worthwhile endeavor.

## Conclusion

Congratulations! You have made it to the end of this book, and by now you should have a clear idea of what is involved in starting and operating a successful photo booth rental business. It takes a lot of hard work and determination. There will be rough times, and times when you are tempted to give up, but if you work through it, you will prevail. People from all walks of life, young and old, will have an amazing time when they step inside your booth, and when they come out, they'll have mementos to keep for years. It's a business this brings a lot of joy to people, and hopefully will bring you lots of success too. I wish you the best of luck, and thank you for taking the time to read this.

Please visit the website for this book at www.photobooth101.com for more information and some free downloads.

www.ingramcontent.com/pod-product-compliance
Lightning Source LLC
Chambersburg PA
CBHW061512180526

45171CB00001B/139